A SUBJECT BIBLIOGRAPHY OF THE SECOND WORLD WAR: BOOKS IN ENGLISH 1975–1983

To the continued memory of
L/C LEONARD A. BAKER,
South Lancashire Regiment
(The Prince of Wales's Volunteers),
who gave his life on D-Day at
Hermanville (Sword Beach), Normandy,
6 June 1944

A SUBJECT BIBLIOGRAPHY
OF THE SECOND WORLD WAR:
BOOKS IN ENGLISH 1975–1983

A. G. S. Enser
FLA FRSA

A Grafton Book

Gower

R

940.53 016

Published by

Gower Publishing Company
Limited,
Gower House, Croft Road,
Aldershot,
Hants GU11 3HR,
England

Gower Publishing Company,
Old Post Road,
Brookfield,
Vermont 05036,
USA

British Library Cataloguing in Publication Data

Enser, A.G.S.
  A subject bibliography of the Second World War:
  books in English 1975—1983 — (A Grafton book)
  1. World War, 1939—1945 — Bibliography
  I. Title
  016.94053   Z6207.W8

  ISBN 0-566-03514-6

Library of Congress Cataloging in Publication Data

Enser, A.G.S.
  A subject bibliography of the Second World War.

  (A Grafton book)
  Includes indexes.
  1. World War, 1939—45 — Bibliography
  I. Title.
  Z6207.W8E58 1984 [D743] 016.940.53 84-13619
  ISBN 0-566-03514-6

Printed and bound in Great Britain by
Biddles Ltd, Guildford and King's Lynn

CARH

CONTENTS

PREFACE

The first volume of *A Subject Bibliography of the Second World War*, comprised books in English published between 1939—1974.

In the United Kingdom, the year 1974 is important for historians, and all interested in World War II because, under the 30 year rule, many previously unrevealed State documents, and reports, dealing with events and personages in 1944, and subsequently, were made available, in the Public Record Office, for open inspection.

The years 1944 and 1945 were of great moment and import to mankind, for example, the Normandy Landings; the strategic bombing of Germany; the Russian Offensives; Victory in Europe; the atom bomb; the American Offensives in the Pacific; and the surrender of Japan.

Consequently, many vital secrets have been disclosed, for example, the British ability to decode and read the German ciphers by *Enigma* and *Ultra*. Similarly, by the Americans, the Japanese codes by *Magic* and *Purple*. Some of the wartime secret activities of the British S.O.E. (Special Operations Executive), and the American O.S.S. (Office of Strategic Service) have been revealed in books published since 1974. Widespread coverage, in the past few years, by cinema, radio and television, with such examples as *World at War, Holocaust* and *Secret War*, has maintained and increased public interest. The sixth of June 1984, as the 40th Anniversary of the D-Day Landings in Normandy, will be remembered, for various reasons, throughout the world.

SCOPE

This second volume covers books in English published between 1975 and 1983. I am indebted to readers and reviewers who kindly informed me of omissions to the original volume. The opportunity has been taken to include such where possible. In general, works of less than thirty pages, poetry, fiction, juvenile literature, humour, cartoons and the publications of the War Graves Commission have been omitted. In the main the entries have been taken from the *Cumulative Book Index*, the *British National Bibliography* and *Whitaker*. Place and date of publication is given where known, as is any change of title in the United Kingdom, United States of America, or in subsequent editions.

ARRANGEMENT

The subject headings are arranged in alphabetical order. Within each subject heading, generally, the entries are also arranged alphabetically by author or title. Exceptions to this are: BRITISH ARMY: MEMOIRS: and UNITED STATES ARMY. For these the arrangements are as follows:

BRITISH ARMY (General); Eighth Army; Fourteenth Army; Twenty-first Army Group; Divisions; Corps; and Regiments (in alphabetical order).

MEMOIRS are arranged alphabetically under the name of the subject, except for major personalities such as Churchill, Montgomery, Patton, Roosevelt or Stalin, who have separate subject headings with *see also* references.

UNITED STATES ARMY (General); Third Army; Fifth Army; Sixth Army; Seventh Army; Divisions (in numerical order).

Major events are given separate subject headings, for example, Arnhem; Bataan; Guadalcanal, with *see also* references to related or wider subject material.

Bibliographical information is minimal but sufficient for

identification. Of course, general agreement in the placing of every entry under a particular subject cannot be expected in a compilation of this nature on such a complex event as the Second World War. However, I have aimed to place each entry where the majority of users could be expected to find it, and I have used double entries where the subject matter appears to justify. It must be emphasised that no claim is made to the entries being exhaustive, and I shall be pleased to be informed of omissions and errors.

ACKNOWLEDGEMENTS

I am indebted to W. Bennett, Librarian of the Local Government Unit of the East Sussex County Libraries, and his staff, for their help in obtaining books for my bibliographical research; to the late James (Jimmie) W. Drawbell for many kindnesses; and in particular, to my wife and family for their forbearance and encouragement.

A.G.S. Enser,
Eastbourne, Sussex,
February 1984

ABBREVIATIONS

Ala	Alabama
Aus	Austria
Aust	Australia
Berks	Berkshire
bib	bibliography
Brit Col	British Columbia
Bucks	Buckinghamshire
Cal	California
comp	compiler
Conn	Connecticut
CUP	Cambridge University Press
Del	Delaware
ed(s)	editor(s)
Eng	England
Fla	Florida
Ga	Georgia
Hants	Hampshire
Herts	Hertfordshire
HMS	His/Her Majesty's Ship
HMSO	His/Her Majesty's Stationery Office
Ill	Illinois
Ind	Indiana
jun	junior
Kty	Kentucky
La	Louisiana
Lancs	Lancashire
Mass	Massachusetts
Md	Maryland
Mich	Michigan
Minn	Minnesota
Mo	Missouri

Mx	Middlesex
NC	North Carolina
NH	New Hampshire
NJ	New Jersey
NM	New Mexico
NSW	New South Wales
NY	New York State
NZ	New Zealand
Okl	Oklahoma
Ont	Ontario
OUP	Oxford University Press
Oxon	Oxfordshire
p	pages
Pa	Pennsylvania
RAF	Royal Air Force
rev ed	revised edition
Salop	Shropshire
SC	South Carolina
Scot	Scotland
Som	Somerset
Sx	Sussex
Sy	Surrey
Tenn	Tennessee
Tex	Texas
UK	United Kingdom
UP	University Press
US	United States of America
USAAF	United States Army Air Force
USMC	United States Marine Corps
USS	United States Ship
unp	unpaged
Va	Virginia
vol	volume
War	Warwickshire
Wilts	Wiltshire
Wis	Wisconsin
Yorks	Yorkshire

SUBJECT BIBLIOGRAPHY

AFRIKA KORPS

BARKER, A J
Afrika Korps *(London: Bison 1978), 192p.*

BENDER, Roger J *and* LAW, Richard D
Uniforms, organization and history of the Afrika Korps *(Mountain View: Author 1973), 253p., bib.*

BERGOT, Erwan
The Afrika Korps *(London: Wingate 1976), 256p., bib.*

BLANCO, Richard L
Rommel, the desert warrior: the Afrika Korps in World War II *(New York: Messner 1982), 191p.*

FORTY, G
Afrika Korps at war *(London: Ian Allan 1978), 2 vols.*

HECKMAN, Wolf
Rommel's war in Africa *(London: Granada 1981), 366p., bib.*

LEWIN, Ronald
The life and death of the Afrika Korps: a biography *(London: Batsford 1977), 207p., bib.*

LUCAS, James S
Panzer Army Africa *(London: Macdonald & Jane's 1977), 211p., bib.*

MITCHAM, Samuel W
Rommel's desert war: the life and death of the Afrika Korps *(New York: Stein & Day 1982), 219p.*

QUARRIE, Bruce
Afrika Korps *(Cambridge, Eng.: Stephens 1975), 64p.*

SCHMIDT, Heinz W
With Rommel in the desert *(London: Harrap 1980), 240p.*

WINDROW, Martin C
Rommel's desert army *(New York: Hippocrene 1976), 40p.*

[see also BRITISH ARMY: EIGHTH ARMY, MIDDLE EAST, NORTH AFRICA, ROMMEL, TANKS]

AIRBORNE FORCES

AIRBORNE Operations: an illustrated encyclopaedia of the great battles of airborne forces *(London: Salamander 1978), 222p.*

ANDERSON, Dudley
Three cheers for the next man to die *(London: Hale 1983), 205p.*

BURGETT, Donald
Currahee! we stand alone: a paratrooper's account of the Normandy invasion *(London: Hutchinson 1967), 142p.*

CROOKENDEN, Napier
Airborne at war *(London: Ian Allan 1978), 144p.*
Dropzone Normandy: the story of the American and British airborne assault on D Day 1944 *(New York: Scribner 1976), 304p.*

DANK, Milton
The glider gang: an eyewitness history of World War II glider combat *(Philadelphia (Pa): Lippincott 1977), 273p.*

DAVIS, Brian L
US airborne forces Europe, 1942—45 *(London: Arms & Armour, 1974), 34p.*

DEVLIN, Gerard
Paratrooper *(London: Robson 1979), 717p. bib.*

DOVER, Victor
The silken canopy *(London: Cassell 1979), 189p.*
The sky generals *(London: Cassell 1981), 215p., bib.*

ELLIS, John
A history of Airborne Command and Airborne Center *(Sharpsburg (Md): Antietam National Museum 1979), 53p.*

FOXALL, Raymond
The guinea pigs: Britain's first parachute raid *(London: Hale 1983), 208p.*

FROST, John
A drop too many *(London: Buchan & Enright: new and enlarged ed. 1982), 271p.*

GAVIN, James M
Airborne warfare *(Uptown Station Nashville, Tenn: Battery 1980), 186p.*
On to Berlin: battles of an airborne commander, 1942—1946 *(New York: Viking 1978), 336p.*

GREGORY, Barry *and* BATCHELOR, J M
Airborne warfare 1918—1945 *(London: Phoebus 1979), 128p.*

HOUSTON, Robert J
D-Day to Bastogne: a paratrooper recalls World War II *(Hickaville, NY: Exposition 1980), 172p.*

HUSTON, James A
Out of the blue: U.S. Army airborne operations in World War II *(Nashville, Tenn: Battery 1972), 327p.*

KATCHER, Philip R N
US 101st Airborne Division, 1942—45 *(London: Osprey 1978), 40p.*

KENT, Roy
First in! Parachute Pathfinder Company: a history of the 21st Independent Parachute Company, the original pathfinders of British Airborne Forces, 1942—1946 *(London: Batsford 1979), 181p., bib.*

KUHN, Volkman
German paratroops in World War II *(London: Ian Allan 1978), 240p.*

McDONALD, Kenneth L
Into the blue *(Palmerston North: (NZ) 1979), 115p.*

McDONOUGH, James L
Sky riders: history of the 327/401 Glider infantry *(Nashville, Tenn: Battery 1980), 162p.*

MRAZEK, James E
Fighting gliders of World War II *(London: Hale 1977), 207p.*
The glider war *(London: Hale 1975), 304p., bib.*

[*see also CRETE, NORMANDY*]

AIRCRAFT CARRIERS

APPS, Michael
The four 'Ark Royals' *(London: Kimber 1976), 256p.*

BELOTE, H *and* BELOTE, W M
Titans of the seas: the development and operations of Japanese and American Carrier Task Forces during World War II *(New York: Harper 1975), 336p.*

BROWN, David
Carrier fighters, 1934—1945 *(London: Macdonald & Jane's 1975), 160p.*

FRANK, P *and* HARRINGTON, J D
Rendezvous at Midway: USS Yorktown and the Japanese Carrier Fleet *(New York: Day 1967), 252p.*

HANSON, Norman
Carrier pilot *(Cambridge: Stephens 1979), 255p.*

KILDUFF, Peter
US Carriers at war *(London: Ian Allan 1981), 128p., bib.*

LINDLEY, John M
Carrier victory: the air war in the Pacific *(New York: Dutton 1978), 184p.*

POOLMAN, Kenneth
Escort Carrier: HMS Vindex at war *(London: Cooper 1983), 216p.*

REESE, Lee F *(comp)*
Men of the blue ghost (USS Lexington CV-16): historical events of World War II in the Pacific *(San Diego, Cal: Lexington 1980), 923p.*

REYNOLDS, Clark G
The Carrier war *(Alexandria, Va: Time-Life 1982), 176p.*
The fast Carriers; the forging of an air Navy *(Huntingdon, NY: Krieger 1968), 502p.*

[*see also MIDWAY, PACIFIC, ROYAL NAVY, US NAVY*]

AIRFIELDS

ACTION Stations: Military airfields in Lincolnshire and the East Midlands *(Cambridge: Stephens 1981), 217p.*

BOWYER, Michael J F
Wartime military airfields of East Anglia, 1939–1945 *(Cambridge: Stephens 1979), 232p.*

RAMSEY, Winston G
Airfields of the Eighth then and now *(London: Battle of Britain Prints International 1978), 240p.*

AIR GUNNERS

BOWYER, Chaz
Guns in the sky: the air gunners of World War II *(London: Dent 1979), 182p., bib.*

AIR WARFARE (general)

ALTIERI, James
The spearheaders: a personal history of Darby's Rangers *(New York: Zenger 1979), 325p.*

ANGELUCCI, Enzo *and* MATRICARDI, P
World War II airplanes *(New York: Rand-McNally 1978)*, *2 vols.*

BAILEY, R H
The air war in Europe *(Alexandria, Va: Time-Life 1979)*, *208p.*

BAVOUSETT, Glean B
More World War II aircraft in combat *(New York: Arco 1981)*, *144p.*

BERLINER, Don
World War Two jet fighters: scale reference data *(Milwaukee, Wis: Kalmbach 1982)*, *72p.*

BOEMAN, John
Morotai: a memoir of war *(New York: Doubleday 1981)*, *278p.*

BOWYER, Chaz
Air war over Europe, 1939—1945 *(London: Kimber 1981)*, *235p., bib.*
Images of air war, 1939—1945 *(London: Batsford 1983)*, *120p. bib.*

CHANT, Christopher
World War II aircraft *(London: Orbis 1975)*, *143p.*

COLLIER, Basil
A history of air power *(London: Weidenfeld & Nicolson 1974)*, *358p., bib.*

COPP, DeWitt S
Forged in fire: strategy and decisions in the airwar over Europe, 1940—45 *(New York: Doubleday 1982)*, *531p.*

FRY, Garry L *and* ETHELL, J L
Escort to Berlin *(New York: Arco 1980)*, *226p.*

GOODSON, James A
Tumult in the clouds *(London: Kimber 1983)*, *238p.*

GUNSTON, Bill
The illustrated encyclopaedia of combat aircraft of World War II *(London: Salamander 1978)*, *261p.*

GURNEY, Gene *ed.*
Great air battles *(New York: Bramhall House 1963), 291p.*

HALL, Roger M D
Clouds of fear *(Folkestone, Kent: Bailey 1975), 187p.*

HANSELL, Haywood S *jun.*
The air plan that defeated Hitler *(New York: Arno 1980), 311p.*

JABLONSKI, Edward
Air war *(New York: Doubleday 1979), 4 vols.*

JACKSON, Robert
Air war over France: May–June 1940 *(London: Ian Allan 1974), 154p.*

LUCAS, Laddie
Wings of war: airmen of all nations tell their stories, 1939–1945 *(London: Hutchinson 1983), 409p.*

NESBITT-DUFORT, John
Scramble: flying the aircraft of World War II *(London: Speed & Sports 1970), 125p.*

OVERY, R J
The air war, 1939–1945 *(London: Europa 1980), 263p., bib.*

PHILPOTT, Bryan
In enemy hands: revealing true stories behind Allied aircraft losses *(Cambridge: Stephens 1981), 89p.*

RUMPF, Hans
The bombing of Germany *(London: White Lion 1975), 256p.*

SHORES, Christopher F
Ground attack aircraft of World War II *(London: Macdonald & Jane's 1977), 191p., bib.*

SUNDERMAN, J F *ed.*
World War II in the air *(New York: Reinhold 1981), 2 vols.*

TAYLOR, Harold A
Test pilot at war *(London: Ian Allan 1970), 144p.*

TIBBETTS, Paul W *and others*
The Tibbetts story *(New York: Stein & Day 1978), 316p.*

ULANOFF, Stanley M *ed*.
World War II aircraft in combat *(New York: Arco 1976), 144p.*

WINGS Of War *(London: Hutchinson 1983), 496p.*

WYPER, William W
The youngest tigers in the sky *(Palos Verdes, Cal: Wyper 1980), 191p.*

ALANBROOKE

FRASER, David
Alanbrooke *(London: Collins 1982), 604p., bib.*

AMIENS RAID

FISHMAN, Jack
And the walls came tumbling down *(London: Souvenir 1982), 448p.*

AMPHIBIOUS WARFARE

DUNN, Walter S
Second Front now—1943 *(University of Alabama 1980), 318p.*

GODSON, Susan H
Viking of assault: Admiral Leslie Hall, jn., and amphibious warfare *(Washington, DC: UP of America 1982), 238p.*

LADD, J D
Assault from the sea, 1939—45: the craft, the landings, the men *(New York: Hippocrene 1976), 256p.*

LUND, Paul *and* LUDLAM, Harry
The war of the landing craft *(London: Foulsham 1976), 256p.*

WHITEHOUSE, Arch
Amphibious operations *(London: Muller 1964), 351p.*

ANTWERP

MOULTON, James L
Battle for Antwerp: the liberation of the city and the opening of the Scheldt, 1944 *(London: Ian Allan 1978), 208p.*

ARDENNES

WHITING, Charles
Death of a Division *(London: Cooper 1979), 158p. bib.*

[*see also BASTOGNE*]

ARMS AND ARMOUR

BARBARSKI, Krzysztof
Polish armour, 1939–45 *(London: Osprey 1982), 40p.*

CONNIFORD, Michael P
British light military trucks, 1939–1945: British-built 5 cwt, 8 cwt and 15 cwt vehicles *(Kings Langley, Bucks: Argus 1976), 88p.*

CULVER; Bruce
The SdKfz 251 half-track *(London: Osprey 1983), 40p.*

ELLIS, Christopher *ed.*
Directory of wheeled vehicles of the Wehrmacht, 1933–45 *(London: Ducimus 1974), 128p.*

FUNCKEN, Liliane
Arms and uniforms: the Second World War *(London: Ward Lock 1975–76), 4 vols.*

GANDER, Terence *and* CHAMBERLAIN, Peter
Small arms, artillery and special weapons of the Third Reich *(London: Macdonald 1979), 352p.*

GROVE, Eric
German armour: Poland and France, 1939—1940 *(London: Almark 1976), 72p.*
Russian armour, 1941—43 *(London: Almark 1977), 72p.*

HOGG, Ian V
The encyclopaedia of infantry weapons of World War II *(London: Arms & Armour 1977), 192p.*

O'NEILL, Richard
Suicide squads: Axis and Allied special attack weapons of World War II: their development and their missions *(London: Salamander 1981), 296p., bib.*

WEEKS, John
World War II small arms *(London: Orbis 1979), 144p.*

ZALOGA, Steven J
Armour of the Pacific war, 1937—45 *(London: Osprey 1983), 40p.*
US half-tracks of World War II *(London: Osprey 1983), 40p.*

[*see also GERMAN ARMY, PANZERS, TANKS*]

ARNHEM

ANGUS, Tom
Men at Arnhem *(London: Cooper 1976), 208p.*

FAIRLEY, John
Remember Arnhem *(London: Pegasus 1978), 235p.*

HEAPS, Leo
The grey goose of Arnhem *(London: Weidenfeld & Nicolson 1976), 245p., bib.*
US title: The evaders.

HORROCKS, *Sir* Brian *and others*
Corps Commander *(London: Sidgwick & Jackson 1977), 256p.*

MAWSON, Stuart R
Arnhem doctor *(London: Orbis 1981), 170p.*

PIEKALKIEWICZ, Janusz
Arnhem 1944 *(London: Ian Allan 1977)*, *112p.*

RYAN, Cornelius
A bridge too far *(London: Hamilton 1974)*, *576p., bib.*

SIMS, James
Arnhem spearhead: a private soldier's story *(London: Imperial War Museum 1978)*, *118p.*

TUGWELL, Maurice
Arnhem: a case study *(London: Thornton Cox 1975)*, *63p., bib.*

ART AND ARTISTS

ARDIZZONE, Edward
Diary of a war artist *(London: Bodley Head 1974)*, *213p.*

BATES, Maxwell B
A wilderness of days: an artist's experiences as a Prisoner of War in Germany *(Victoria, British Col, Sono Nis 1978)*, *133p.*

DE JAEGER, Charles
The Linz file: Hitler's plunder of Europe's art *(London: Webb & Bower 1982)*, *192p.*

JONES, James
W W II: graphics direction *(London: Cooper 1975)*, *272p., bib.*

WEBER, John P
The German war artists *(Fort Buchan, P.R.: Cerburus 1979)*, *151p.*

ARTILLERY

BIDWELL, Shelford
Artillery tactics, 1939—1945 *(London: Almark 1976)*, *72p.*

CHAMBERLAIN, Peter *and* GANDER, T
Anti-aircraft guns *(London: Macdonald & Jane's 1975), 64p.*
Heavy artillery *(London: Macdonald & Jane's 1975), 64p.*

CHAMBERLAIN, Peter *and* MILSOM, John
Self-propelled and anti-tank and anti-aircraft guns *(London: Macdonald & Jane's 1975), 64p.*

HOGG, Ian V
Barrage: the guns in action *(New York: Ballantine 1970), 160p.*
British and American artillery of World War Two *(London: Arms & Armour 1978), 256p.*
German artillery of World War II *(London: Arms & Armour 1975), 304p.*
The guns of World War II *(London: Macdonald & Jane's 1976), 152p., bib.*

MEAD, Peter
Gunners at war, 1939—1945 *(London: Ian Allan 1982), 128p., bib.*

ATOM BOMB

AKIZUKI, Tatsuichiro
Nagasaki 1945: the first full-length witness account of the atomic bomb attack on Nagasaki *(London: Quartet 1981), 158p.*

BUSH, Vannevar
Pieces of the action *(New York: Morrow 1970), 366p.*

CAVE-BROWN, Anthony *and* McDONALD, C B *eds.*
The secret history of the atomic bomb *(New York: Dial 1977), 582p.*

CHILDREN of Hiroshima *(London: Taylor & Francis 1980), 333p.*

CRONDON, Edmund D *and* ROSENOF, T *comps.*
The Second World War and the atomic age, 1940—1973 *(Northbrook, Ill: AHM 1975), 146p.*

GALLAGHER, Thomas
Assault in Norway *(London: Macdonald & Jane's 1975)*, *238p. (Later published as:* The Telemark raid.*)*

HIRSCHFELD, Burt
A cloud over Hiroshima: the story of the atomic bomb *(New York: Messner 1967)*, *179p., bib.*

INTERNATIONAL Symposium on the damage and after-effects of the atomic bombing of Hiroshima and Nagasaki *(Tokyo: Asahi 1978)*, *264p., bib.*

IRVING, David
The virus house *(London: Kimber 1967)*, *288p.*

RICHARDSON, Cordell
Uranium trail East *(London: Bachman & Turner 1977)*, *144p.*

SHERWIN, Martin J
A world destroyed: the atomic bomb and the Grand Alliance *(New York: Knopf 1975)*, *315p.*

THOMAS, Gordon *and* WITTS, M
Ruin from the air: the atomic mission to Hiroshima *(London: Hamilton 1977)*, *386p. US title:* 'Enola Gay'

AUCHINLECK

PARKINSON, Roger
The Auk: Auchinleck victor at Alamein *(London: Hart-Davis MacGibbon 1977)*, *272p., bib.*

AUSTRALIA

BELL, Ken
Not in vain *(Melbourne, Aust: Wren 1973)*, *141p.*

BELL, Roger J
Unequal allies: Australia—American relations and the Pacific war *(Carlton, Victoria, Aust: Melbourne UP 1977)*, *278p.*

CARR-GREGG, Charlotte
Japanese prisoners of war in revolt: the outbreaks at Featherstone and Cowra during World War II *(London: St Martins 1978), 225p.*

MOORE, John H
Over-sexed, over-paid and over here: Americans in Australia, 1941—1945 *(Brisbane, Aust: UP Queensland 1981), 303p.*

AUSTRALIAN AIR FORCE

ANDERSON, Peter N
Mustangs of the RAAF and RNZAF *(Sydney, Aust: Reed 1975), 103p. bib.*

AUSTRALIAN ARMY

COOMBE, Gilchrist
2/48th Australian Infantry Battalion *(Adelaide, Aust: 2/48th AIF 1972)*

HORNER, D M
Crisis of command: Australian generalship and the Japanese threat, 1941—1943 *(Canberra, Aust: Australian National UP 1978), 395p.*

HORTON, Dick
Ring of fire: Australian guerilla operations against the Japanese forces in World War II *(London: Cooper 1983), 164p.*

MACKIE, Ronald
Echoes from forgotten wars *(London: Collins 1980), 269p.*

PAULL, Raymond
Retreat from Kokoda: Australian campaign in New Guinea *(London: Cooper 1983)*

AUSTRALIAN NAVY

GILLISON, Douglas
Royal Australian Navy, 1942—1945 *(Canberra, Aust: Australian War Memorial 1968)*

MONTGOMERY, Michael
Who sank the Sydney? *(London: Cooper, rev. & enl. ed. 1983), 242p.*

AUSTRIA

BUTTERWORTH, Emma M
As the waltz was ending *(New York: Four Winds 1982), 187p.*

GOLDNER, Franz
Austrian emigration, 1938—1945 *(New York: Ungar 1979), 212p.*

MAASS, David
Country without a name: Austria under Nazi rule, 1938—1945 *(New York: Ungar 1979), 178p.*

BADGES

DAVIS, Brian
Badges and insignia of the Third Reich, 1933—1945 *(Poole, Dorset: Blandford 1983), 160p.*

ROSIGNOLI, Guido
Army badges and insignia of World War 2, Book 2: British Commonwealth, Canada, South Africa, British African Territories, India, British Overseas Territories, Finland, France, Japan, Netherlands, Yugoslavia, China, Denmark, Czechoslovakia *(Poole, Dorset: Blandford 1975), 198p.*

TUNBRIDGE, Frederick C
Badges and medals of the Third Reich *(Larkhall, Lanarkshire, the Author 1976), 27p.*

BALLOONS

MIKESH, Robert C
Balloon bomb attacks on North America: Japan's World War II assaults *(Fallbrook, Cal: Aero 1982), 84p.*

BASTOGNE

CROOKENDEN, *Sir* Napier
Battle of the bulge, 1944 *(London: Ian Allan 1980), 160p.*

MARSHALL, S L A
Bastogne: the story of the first eight days in which the 101st Airborne Division was closed within the ring of German Forces *(Washington, DC: Zenger 1979), 261p.*

ZALOGA, Steven J
Battle of the bulge *(London: Arms & Armour 1983), 64p.*

BATAAN

KNOX, Donald
Death march: the survivors of Bataan *(New York: Harcourt 1981), 482p.*

MACHI, Mario
The Emperor's hostages *(New York: Vantage 1982), 90p.*

MALLONEE, Richard C
The naked flagpole: battle for Bataan *(Novato, Cal: Presidio 1980), 204p.*

SCHULTZ, Duane P
Hero of Bataan: the story of General Jonathan M. Wainwright *(New York: St Martin's 1981), 479p.*

[*see also PHILIPPINES, US MARINE CORPS*]

BATTLE OF BRITAIN

ALLEN, Hubert R
Fighter squadron: a memoir, 1940—1942 *(London: Kimber 1979), 192p.*

COLLIER, Basil
Leader of the Few: the authorized biography of Air Chief Marshal the Lord Dowding *(London: Jarrolds 1957), 264p.*

COLLYER, David G
Battle of Britain diary: July—September 1940 *(Deal, Kent: Kent Defence Research 1980), 120p., bib.*

COOKSLEY, Peter
Defend the heart *(London: Hale 1983), 224p.*

DEIGHTON, Len
Battle of Britain *(London: Cape 1980), 224p.*
Fighter: the true story of the Battle of Britain *(London: Cape 1977), 304p., bib.*

FRANKS, Norman L R
Wings of freedom: Twelve Battle of Britain pilots *(London: Kimber 1980), 205p., bib.*

GOLDSMITH-CARTER, George
The Battle of Britain *(London: Mason & Lipscomb 1974), 279p., bib.*

GREEN, William
Aircraft of the Battle of Britain *(London: Macdonald 1969), 64p.*

ISHOVEN, Armand van
The Luftwaffe in the Battle of Britain *(London: Ian Allan 1980), 128p.*

JACKSON, Robert
Squadron-scramble: yeoman of the Battle of Britain *(London: Barker 1978), 141p.*

JOHNSTONE, A U R [Sandy]
Enemy in the sky: my 1940 diary *(London: Kimber 1976), 191p.*

KENT, John A
One of the few *(London: Kimber 1971), 254p.*

KNIGHT, Dennis
Harvest of Messerschmitts: the chronicle of a village at war *(London: Warne 1981), 183p.*

MOSLEY, Leonard
Battle of Britain *(Alexandria, Va: Time-Life 1977), 208p.*

MUNSON, Kenneth *and* TAYLOR, John *eds.*
The Battle of Britain *(London: New English Library 1976), 128p.*

PRICE, Alfred
Battle of Britain: the hardest day, 18th August 1940 *(London: Macdonald & Jane's 1979), 223p., bib.*

STANHOPE-PALMER, Robert
Tank trap 1940, or, No battle in Britain *(Ilfracombe, Devon: Stockwell 1976), 205p., bib.*

TILBURY, Ann
The Battle of Britain *(London: Macdonald 1981), 61p.*

WARD, Richard
Battle of Britain: Hawker Hurricane, Supermarine Spitfire, Messerschmitt Bf.109 *(London: Osprey 1969), 40p.*

WOOD, Derek *comp.*
Target England: an illustrated history of the Battle of Britain *(London: Jane's 1980), 192p.*

BATTLES (general)

DUPUY, Trevor *and* MARTELL, Paul
Great battles on the Eastern Front: the Soviet-German war 1941−1945 *(Minneapolis: Bobbs-Merrill 1982), 249p.*

GOODENOUGH, Simon
War maps: great land, sea and air battles of World War II *(London: Macdonald 1982), 192p., bib.*

MAULE, Henry
The great battles of World War II *(New York: Galahad 1976), 448p.*

PRESTON, Anthony *ed.*
Decisive battles of Hitler's wars *(London: Hamlyn 1977), 256p.*

BATTLESHIPS

BROWN, David
Tirpitz: the floating fortress *(London: Arms & Armour 1977), 160p.*

DULIN, Robert O *and* GARZKE, W H
Battleships: United States battleships in World War II *(London: Macdonald & Jane's 1976), 267p.*

JONES, Geoffrey
Battleship Barham *(London: Kimber 1979), 272p.*

KEMP, Peter K
The escape of the Scharnhorst and Gneisenau *(London: Ian Allan 1975), 96p.*

MIDDLEBROOK, Martin *and* MAHONEY, Patrick
Battleship: the loss of the Prince of Wales and the Repulse *(London: Lane 1977), 366p., bib.*

MULLENHEIM-RECHBERG, Burkhard
Battleship Bismarck: a survivor's story *(Annapolis, Md: Naval Institute 1980), 334p.*

SMITH, Peter C
The great ships pass: British battleships at war, 1939—1945 *(London: Kimber 1977), 544p.*
Hit first, hit hard: HMS Renown, 1916—1948 *(London: Kimber 1979), 335p.*

SNYDER, Gerald S
The 'Royal Oak' disaster *(London: Kimber 1976), 240p., bib.*

SPURR, Russell
A glorious way to die: the kamikaze mission of the battleship Yamato, April 1945 *(New York: Newmarket 1981),
341p.*

VETTERS, Heinz O *and* Coz, R
Battleships of the US Navy in World War II *(New York:
Crown 1979), 131p.*

WINTON, John
The death of the Scharnhorst *(Chichester, Sx: Bird 1983),
236p.*

[*see also* NAVIES OF INDIVIDUAL COUNTRIES]

BELGIUM

RENAULT-ROULIER, Gilbert
The eighteenth day: the tragedy of King Leopold III of
Belgium *(New York: Everest House 1978), 348p.*

[*see also* RESISTANCE]

BERLIN

ETHELL, Jeffrey *and* PRICE, Alfred
Target Berlin: Mission 250, 6 March 1944 *(London:
Macdonald & Jane's 1981), 212p., bib.*

O'DONNELL, James
The Berlin bunker *(London: Dent 1979), 317p.*

BIBLIOGRAPHIES

BAYLISS, G M
Bibliographical guide to the two World Wars: an annotated
survey of English language reference materials *(New York:
Bowker 1977), 578p.*

BLOOMBERG, M
The Jewish holocaust: an annotated guide to books in
English *(New York: Borgo 1982), 192p.*

COCHRAN, Alexander S
The MAGIC diplomatic summaries *(New York: Garland
1982), 139p.*

ENSER, A G S
A subject bibliography of the Second World War: books in
English, 1939—1974 *(London: Deutsch 1977), 592p.*

FUNK, Arthur L *ed.*
A select bibliography of books on the Second World War
published in the US 1966—75 *(New York: MA—AH 1978)*

SMITH, Myron J *jun.*
World War II at sea: a bibliography of sources in English
(Metuchen, NJ: Scarecrow, 1976), 3 vols.

**BLITZ ON UNITED KINGDOM
(APART FROM LONDON)**

HARRISSON, Tom
Living through the Blitz *(London: Collins 1976), 372p.,
bib.*

PRICE, Alfred
Blitz on Britain: the bomber attacks on the United
Kingdom, 1939—1945 *(London: Ian Allan 1977), 192p.*

BLOCKADE

BARKER, Ralph
The blockade busters *(London: Chatto & Windus 1976),
224p., bib.*

BRICE, Martin H
Axis blockade runners of World War II *(London: Batsford
1981), 159p.*

HAMPSHIRE, Arthur C
The blockaders *(London: Kimber 1980), 224p., bib.*

LEASOR, James
Boarding party *(London: Heinemann 1978), 240p. (Later published as:* The sea wolves.*)*

BOMBERS (Allied)

ARDERBY, Philip
Bomber pilot: a memoir of World War II *(Lexington, Kty: University of Kentucky 1978), 233p.*

BENDINER, Elmer
The fall of fortresses: a personal account of the most daring — and deadly — American air battles of World War II *(New York: Putnam 1980), 258p.*

BIRDSALL, Steve
B-17 in action *(Warren, Mich: Squadron/Signal 1973), 50p.*
B-24 Liberator in action *(Warren, Mich: Squadron/Signal 1975), 50p.*
B-29 Superfortress *(Warren, Mich: Squadron/Signal 1977), 48p.*
Saga of the Superfortress: the dramatic story of the B-29 and the Twentieth Air Force *(London: Sidgwick & Jackson 1982), 346p.*

BLUE, Allan G
The B-24 Liberator: a pictorial history *(London: Ian Allan 1976), 223p.*

BOWMAN, Martin
The B-24 Liberator, 1939—1945 *(Norwich, Norfolk: Wensum 1979), 128p.*

BOWYER, Chaz
Bomber barons *(London: Kimber 1983), 222p.*
Bomber Group at war *(London: Ian Allan 1981), 160p., bib.*
Hampden special *(London: Ian Allan 1975), 64p.*
Wellington at war *(London: Ian Allan 1982), 128p., bib.*

BOWYER, Michael J F
The Stirling bomber *(London: Faber 1979), 240p.*

BRADLEY, Catherine *ed.*
B-29 Superfortress *(Yeovil, Som: Haynes 1983), 56p.*

BROOKES, Andrew
Bomber squadron at war *(London: Ian Allan 1983), 144p., bib.*

CAIDIN, Martin
Flying Forts *(New York: Ballantine 1979), 504p.*

COFFEY, Thomas M
Decision over Schweinfurt: the US 8th Air Force battle for daylight bombing *(London: Hale 1978), 373p.*

COOPER, Alan W
Beyond the dams to the Tirpitz *(London: Kimber 1983).*
The men who breached the dams *(London: Kimber 1982), 223p.*

COOPER, Bryan
The story of the bomber, 1914—1945 *(London: Octopus 1974), 124p.*

CURRIE, Jack
Lancaster target *(London: New English Library 1977), 175p.*

FREEMAN, Roger A
The US strategic bomber *(London: Macdonald & Jane's 1975), 160p., bib.*
B-17 Fortress at war *(London: Ian Allan 1977), 192p.*
B-24 Liberator at war *(London: Ian Allan 1983), 128p.*
B-26 Marauder at war *(London: Ian Allan 1978), 192p.*

GARBETT, Mike *and* GOULDING, Brian
The Lancaster at war *(London: Ian Allan 1979), 176p.*
Lincoln at war, 1944—1966 *(London: Ian Allan 1979), 174p.*

GOMERSALL, Bryce *comp.*
The Stirling file *(Tonbridge, Kent: Air-Britain 1979), 95p.*

GOULDING, James *and* MOYES, P J
R.A.F. Bomber Command and its aircraft, 1941—
(London: Ian Allan 1975—78), 2 vols.

A GUIDE to the reports of the United States strategic bombing survey *(Woodbridge, Sy: Boydell 1981), 224p.*

GUNSTON, Bill
An illustrated guide to bombers of World War II *(New York: Arco 1980), 160p.*

HASTINGS, Max
Bomber Command *(London: Joseph 1979), 399p., bib.*

HENDRIE, Andrew
Seek and strike: the Lockheed Hudson *(London: Kimber 1983)*

HESS, William N
A-20 Boston at war *(London: Ian Allan 1979), 128p.*
US title: A-20 Havoc at war.
B-17 Flying Fortress *(New York: Ballantine 1974).*
P-47 Thunderbolt at war *(London: Ian Allan 1976), 160p.*

JACKSON, Robert
Bomber!: famous bomber missions of World War II *(London: Barker 1980), 157p.*

JOHNSEN, Frederick A
The bomber barons: the history of the 5th Bomb Group in the Pacific during World War II *(Tacoma, Wash: Bomber 1982), vol.I.*

JOHNSON, Brian
Night bombers *(London: Thames Methuen 1983), 272p.*

JONES, Geoffrey P
Attacker: the Hudson and its flyers *(London: Kimber 1980), 238p.*
Night flight: Halifax squadrons at war *(London: Kimber 1981), 224p.*
Raider: the Halifax and its flyers *(London: Kimber 1978), 240p.*

JONES, William E
Bomber intelligence: 103, 150, 166, 170 Squadron operations and techniques 1942–1945 *(Leicester: Midland Counties 1983), 304p.*

KENNETT, Lee B
A history of strategic bombing *(New York: Scribner 1982), 222p.*

LAY, Beirne
Presumed dead: the survival of a bomb group commander *(New York: Dodd, Mead 1980), 140p. (Originally published as:* I've had it.*)*

LONGMATE, Norman
The bombers: the RAF offensive against Germany, 1939–1945 *(London: Hutchinson 1983), 415p.*

LUMSDEN, Alec
Wellington special *(London: Ian Allan 1975), 96p.*

MERRICK, K A
Halifax: an illustrated history of a classic World War 2 bomber *(London: Ian Allan 1980), 224p.*

MORRISON, Wilbur H
Fortress without a roof: the Allied bombing of the Third Reich *(New York: St Martin's 1982), 322p.*

MOYES, Philip J R
Royal Air Force bombers of World War II *(Chalfont St Giles, Bucks: Lacy), 3 vols.*

MUNSON, Kenneth G
Bombers, patrol and transport aircraft, 1939–45 *(London: Blandford 1969), 163p.*

NALTY, Bernard C *and* BERGER, C
The men who bombed the Reich *(New York: Dutton 1978), 184p.*

NESBIT, Roy C
Woe to the unwary: a memoir of low level bombing operations 1941 *(London: Kimber 1981), 192p.*

NESS, William N
A-20 Boston at war *(London: Ian Allan 1979), 128p.*

NEWBY, Leroy W
Target Ploesti: view from a bombsight *(London: Arms & Armour 1983), 288p.*

PASSMORE, Richard
Blenheim boy *(London: Harmsworth 1981), 254p.*

PHILPOTT, B
RAF bomber units, 1939—42 *(London: Osprey 1977), 48p.*

PRICE, Alfred
The bomber in World War II *(London: Macdonald & Jane's 1976), 150p.*

RALEY, Norman
Destination unknown *(Bognor Regis, Sx: New Horizon 1983), 175p.*

RAYMOND, Robert S
A Yank in Bomber Command *(Newton Abbot, Devon: David & Charles 1977), 159p.*

RENAUT, Michael
Terror by night: a bomber pilot's story *(London: Kimber 1982), 192p.*

RUMPF, Hans
The bombing of Germany *(London: White Lion 1975), 256p.*

SAWYER, Tom
Only owls and bloody fools fly at night *(London: Kimber 1982), 191p.*

SCUTTS, Jerry
B-25 Mitchell at war *(London: Ian Allan 1983), 144p.*

SEARBY, J
Essen *(Chippenham, Wilts: Nutshell 1978), 94p.*

SMITH, Arthur C
Halifax crew: the story of a wartime bomber crew *(Stevenage, Herts: Carlton 1983), 60p., bib.*

STREETLY, Martin
Confound and destroy: 100 Group and the bomber support campaign *(London: Macdonald & Jane's 1978), 279p., bib.*

WAINWRIGHT, John
Tail-end Charlie *(London: Macmillan 1978), 187p.*

WHEELER, Keith
Bombers over Japan *(Alexandria, Va: Time-Life 1982), 208p.*

WILLMOTT, Hedley P
B-17 Flying Fortress *(London: Arms & Armour 1980), 64p.*

BORMANN

LANG, Jochim von
Bormann: the man who manipulated Hitler *(London: Weidenfeld & Nicolson 1979), 430p., bib.*

BRAZIL

HILTON, Stanley E
Hitler's secret war in South America, 1939–1945: German military espionage and Allied counter-espionage in Brazil *(Baton Rouge, La: Louisiana State UP 1981), 353p., bib.*

BRITAIN

BEAUMONT, Joan
Comrades in arms: British aid to Russia, 1941–1945 *(London: Davis-Poynter 1980), 264p., bib.*

BRIGGS, Susan
The Home Front: war years in Britain, 1939–1945 *(London: Weidenfeld & Nicolson 1975), 256p.*

CHAMBERLIN, E R
Life in wartime Britain *(London: Batsford 1972), 190p., bib.*

COWLING, Maurice
The impact of Hitler: British politics and British policy, 1933—1940 *(Cambridge: Cambridge UP 1975), 561p., bib.*

HODGSON, Vera
Few eggs and no oranges: a diary showing how unimportant people in London and Birmingham lived through the war years, 1940—45 *(London: Dobson 1976), 480p.*

INGLIS, Brian *and* GRUNDY, B
All our yesterdays: how the newsreels saw them from Munich to the Berlin airlift *(London: Orbis 1974), 128p.*

JOHNSON, Derek E
East Anglia at war, 1939—1945 *(Norwich, Norfolk: Jarrolds 1978), 160p.*

KESSLER, Leo
Yorkshire at war: the story of fighting Yorkshire at home and abroad, 1939—1945 *(Clapham, Yorks: Dalesman 1980), 112p.*

McLAINE, Ian
Ministry of morale: home front morale and the Ministry of Information in World War II *(London: Allen & Unwin 1979), 325p., bib.*

MONHAM, Kathleen
Growing up in World War II *(Hove, Sx: Wayland 1979), 96p., bib.*

MOYNIHAN, Michael *ed.*
People at war, 1939—1945 *(Newton Abbot, Devon: David & Charles 1974), 216p.*

MURPHY, John
Dorset at war *(Shelborne, Dorset: Dorset 1979), 302p.*

NORTHAMPTONSHIRE at war, 1939—1945: a selection of photographs *(Northants: County Library 1978), 144p.*

ROTHWELL, Victor
Britain and the cold war, 1941—1947 *(London: Cape 1982), 551p.*

TRESCATHERIC, B *and* HUGHES, D
Barrow at war *(Chorley, Lancs: Countryside 1979), 48p.*

BRITISH ARMY (general)

BARRINGTON-WHYTE, James
The great tribulation *(Bognor Regis, Sx: New Horizon 1983), 214p.*

BEACH, G R
The task supreme *(Bognor Regis, Sx: New Horizon 1983), 232p.*

BROWN, Archie
Destiny *(Bognor Regis, Sx: New Horizon 1979), 125p.*

CHANT, Christopher
Ground attack *(London: Almark 1976), 72p.*

CRAIG, Norman
The broken plume: a platoon commander's story, 1940—45 *(London: Imperial War Museum 1982), 191p.*

DAVIS, Brian L
British Army uniforms and insignia of World War Two *(London: Arms & Armour 1983), 228p.*

DIXON, Norman
The psychology of military incompetence *(London: Cape 1976), 448p.*

ELLIS, John
The sharp end of war: the fighting man in World War II *(Newton Abbot, Devon: David & Charles 1980), 396p., bib.*

FARRAR-HOCKLEY, Anthony
Infantry tactics *(London: Almark 1976), 72p.*

FRASER, David
And shall we shock them *(London: Hodder & Stoughton 1983), 448p.*

HOWARTH, Harry
Where fate leads *(Bolton, Lancs: Ross Anderson 1983), 272p.*

SCRIVEN, Gordon J
Called up: A tribute to the conscript soldiers during World War II, 1939—1945 *(Weymouth, Dorset: Scriven 1976), 46p.*

WARNER, Philip
Phantom *(London: Kimber 1982), 218p., bib.*

WILLIS, Donald
Eggshells and tea-leaves *(Oxford: Dugdale 1981), 220p.*

(Eighth Army)

MERRITT, Maurice
Eighth Army driver *(Tunbridge Wells, Kent: Midas 1981), 181p.*

SANDARS, John
8th Army in the desert *(Cambridge: Stephens 1976), 64p.*

TUKER, *Sir* Francis
Approach to battle: a commentary *(London: Cassell 1963), 410p.*

(XIV Army)

FORTY, George
XIV Army at war *(London: Ian Allan 1982), 144p., bib.*

(21st Army Group)

NORTH-West Europe, 1944—1945: the achievement of 21st Army Group *(London: HMSO 1953), 270p.*

(Divisions)

GRANT, Roderick
The 51st Highland Division at war *(London: Ian Allan 1977), 160p.*

SANDARS, John
British Guards Armoured Division, 1941–45 *(London: Osprey 1979), 40p.*

(Corps)

Royal Army Medical Corps PETTY, Gerald F
Mad Gerry: Welsh wartime medical officer: a true story by a major in the Royal Army Medical Corps, 1939–1945 *(Newport, Wales: Starling 1982), 143p.*

(Regiments)

Ayrshire Yeomanry (Earl of Carrick's Own)
BROWNLIE, W S
The proud trooper: the history of Ayrshire (Earl of Carrick's Own) Yeomanry *(London: Collins 1964), 639p.*

Devon Regiment ANDERSON, Dudley
Three cheers for the next man to die *(London: Hale), 189p.*

King's Own Scottish Borderers BAGGALEY, J R P
The 6th (Border) Battalion the King's Own Scottish Borderers, 1939–1945 *(Berwick-on-Tweed 1964)*

King's Shropshire Light Infantry RADCLIFFE, G L Y
History of the 2nd Battalion King's Shropshire Light Infantry *(Oxford: Blackwell 1957)*

Northamptonshire Yeomanry BEVAN, D G
The First and Second Northamptonshire Yeomanry, 1934–45 *(Meyer, Brunswick, Germany 1946)*

Queen's Own Cameron Highlanders COCHRANE, P
Charlie Company: in service with C Company, 2nd Queen's Own Cameron Highlanders, 1940—1944 *(London: Chatto & Windus 1977), 179p.*

Royal Artillery SMALL, Bernard
The reluctant gunner *(Aberdeen, Scot: Aberdeen UP 1983), 554p.*

Royal Tank Regiment LIDDELL HART, B H
The tanks: the history of the Royal Tank Regiment *(London: Cassell 1959), vol.2 1939—1945*

ROACH, Peter
The 8.15 to war: memories of a Desert Rat: El Alamein, Wadi Halfa, Tunis, Salerno, Garigliano, Normandy and Holland *(London: Cooper & Secker & Warburg 1982), 184p.*

Seaforth Highlanders BULTERECK, A
Sans peur: history of the 5th Seaforth Highlanders, 1942—5 *(Edinburgh: Mackay 1946)*

Royal Wiltshire Yeomanry PLATT, J R
The Royal Wiltshire Yeomanry (Prince of Wales's Own), 1907—1967 *(London: Garnstone 1972), 272p.*

BULGARIA

MILLER, Marshall L
Bulgaria during the Second World War *(Stanford, Cal: Stanford UP 1975), 290p.*

BURMA

BATY, John A
Surgeon in the jungle war *(London: Kimber 1979), 196p.*

BEAUMONT, Winifred H
A detail on the Burma Front *(London: BBC 1977), 160p.*

BIDWELL, Shelford
Operation Thursday *(London: Hodder & Stoughton 1979), 256p.*

BOWEN, John
Undercover in the jungle *(London: Kimber 1979), 206p.*

BRADLEY, James
Towards the setting sun: an escape from the Thailand—Burma railway, 1943 *(London: Phillimore 1982), 139p.*

CALLAHAN, Raymond
Burma, 1942—1945 *(London: Davis-Poynter 1978), 190p.*

CLIFFORD, Francis
Desperate journey *(London: Hodder & Stoughton 1979), 192p.*

COOPER, Raymond
'B' Company, 9th Battalion, the Border Regiment, 48 Brigade, 17 Indian (Light) Division, IV Corps, 14th Army, S.E. Asia Command: one man's war in Burma, 1942—44 *(London: Dobson 1978), 152p.*

DUNLOP, Richard
Behind Japanese lines: with the OSS in Burma *(Chicago: Rand McNally: 1979), 194p.*

FINNERTY, John T
All quiet on the Irrawaddy *(Bognor Regis, Sx: New Horizon 1979), 225p.*

FORTY, George
XIV Army at war *(London: Ian Allan 1982), 144p., bib.*

HOTZ, R B *and others*
With General Chennault: the story of the Flying Tigers *(New York: Coward-McCann 1943), 276p.*

IRWIN, Anthony
Burmese outpost *(London: Collins 1945), 160p.*

NALTY, Bernard C
Tigers over Asia *(New York: Dutton 1978), 182p.*

PERRETT, Bryan
Tank tracks to Rangoon *(London: Hale 1977), 208p.*

RODRIGUEZ, Helen
  Helen of Burma *(London: Collins 1983), 192p.*

SCROGGS, Dick
  The soapman and the railroad of death *(New York: Dorrance 1976), 85p.*

SHEIL-SMALL, Denis
  Green shadows: a Gurkha story *(London: Kimber 1982), 198p.*

SLATER, R
  Guns through Arcady: Burma and the Burma Road *(Sydney, Aust: Angus & Robertson 1942), 239p.*

SMITH, Eric D
  Battle for Burma *(London: Batsford 1979), 190p.*

TOLAND, John
  The flying tigers *(New York: Dell 1979), 176p.*

TURNBULL, Patrick
  Battle of the box *(London: Ian Allan 1979), 144p.*

WHELAN, R
  The flying tigers *(London: Macdonald 1943), 136p.*

CAEN

MAULE, Henry
  Caen: the brutal battle and the break-out from Normandy *(Newton Abbot, Devon: David & Charles 1977), 160p.*

CAMOUFLAGE

BOWYER, Michael J F
  Fighting colours, RAF fighter camouflage and markings, 1937—1975 *(Cambridge: PSL 1975), 204p.*
  RAF camouflage of World War 2 *(Cambridge: Stephens 1975), 64p.*

BRITISH aviation colours of World War Two: the official camouflage and markings of RAF aircraft, 1939—1945 *(London: Arms & Armour 1976), 56p.*

CRUICKSHANK, Charles
Deception in World War II *(Oxford: Oxford UP 1979), 248p., bib.*

CULVER, Bruce
Panzer colours: camouflage of the German panzer forces, 1939—45 *(London: Arms & Armour 1976), 95p.*

ELLIS, Chris
United States Navy warship camouflage, 1939—1945 *(Henley-on-Thames, Oxon: Kristall, 1975), 549p.*

FREEMAN, Roger A
Camouflage and markings, United States Army Air Force *(London: Ducimus 1974), 240p., bib.*

PHILPOTT, Bryan
Luftwaffe camouflage of World War II *(Cambridge: Stephens 1975), 64p.*

REIT, Seymour
Masquerade: the amazing camouflage deceptions of World War II *(London: Hale 1979), 255p.*

SCUTTS, Jerry
United States Army Air Force camouflage of World War II *(Cambridge: Stephens 1976), 64p.*

CAMPAIGNS

COOK, Graeme
Rescue *(London: Hart-Davis 1978), 142p.*

GREAT Campaigns of World War II *(London: Phoebus 1980), 320p.*

CANADA

BROADFOOT, Barry *ed.*
Six war years, 1939–1945: memories of Canadians at home and abroad *(New York: Doubleday 1975), 417p.*
Years of sorrow, years of shame: the story of the Japanese Canadians in World War II *(Markham, Ontario: Paper-jacks 1979), 370p.*

DORWARD, David
The gold cross: one man's window on the war *(Toronto: Stage & Arts 1978), 92p.*

DOUGLAS, William *and* GREENHOUS, B
Out of the shadows: Canada in the Second World War *(Toronto: OUP 1977), 288p.*

DUNKELMAN, Ben
Dual allegiance *(Toronto: Macmillan 1978), 275p.*

GALLOWAY, Strome
The General who never was *(Belleville, Ont: Mika 1981), 296p.*

MUNRO, Iain R
Canada and the World War *(New York: Wiley 1979), 96p.*

ROBERTSON, Heather *ed.*
A terrible beauty: the art of Canada at war *(Ottawa: National Museum of Canada 1977), 239p.*

SANTOR, Donald M
Canadians at war, 1939–1945 *(New York: Prentice-Hall 1979), 48p.*

CANADIAN AIR FORCE

ALCORN, Douglas
From hell to breakfast *(Toronto: Intruder 1980), 359p.*

ALLISON, Leslie
Canadians in the Royal Air Force *(Roland, Manitoba: Allison 1978), 216p.*

HALLIDAY, Hugh
No.242 Squadron, the Canadian years: the story of the RAF's 'All Canadian' fighter squadron *(Ontario: Canada's Wings 1981), 177p., bib.*
The tumbling sky *(Stittsville, Ontario: Canada's Wings 1978), 324p.*

HEAPS, Leo
The grey goose of Arnhem *(London: Weidenfeld & Nicolson 1976), 295p., bib.*
US title: The evaders

I'LL never forget: Canadian aviation in the Second World War *(Ottawa: Canadian History Society 1979), 96p.*

McINTOSH, Dave
Terror in the starboard seat *(New York: Beaufort 1980), 184p.*

PEDEN, David M
A thousand shall fall *(Stittsville, Ontario: Canada's Wings 1979), 472p.*

THURSTON, Arthur
Bluenose Spitfire *(Hantsport, Nova Scotia: Lancelot 1979), 92p.*

CANADIAN ARMY

NICHOLSON, G W L
The Canadians in Italy, 1943–45 *(Ottawa: Cloutier 1956)*

WHITEHEAD, William
Dieppe 1942 *(Glasgow: Drew 1982), 91p.*

CANADIAN NAVY

LAMB, James B
The corvette Navy: true stories from Canada's Atlantic war *(Toronto: Macmillan 1977), 179p.*

LAWRENCE, Harold
A bloody war: one man's memories of the Canadian Navy, 1939—45 *(Toronto: Macmillan 1979), 193p.*

SWETTENHAM, John
Canada's Atlantic war *(Sarasola, Fla: Samuel-Stevens 1979), 154p.*

CANARIS

BRISSAUD, Andre
Canaris: the biography of Admiral Canaris, chief of German military intelligence in the Second World War *(London: Weidenfeld & Nicolson 1973), 347p., bib.*

HOHNE, Heinz
Canaris *(London: Secker & Warburg 1979), 703p.*

WEST, Nigel
MI 6, British secret intelligence operations, 1900—45 *(London: Weidenfeld & Nicolson 1983)*

CASSINO

KONSALIK, Heinz G
They fell from the sky *(Henley-on-Thames, Oxon: Ellis 1977), 210p.*

PIEKALKIEWICZ, Janusz
Cassino: anatomy of the battle *(London: Orbis 1980), 192p.*

SMITH, Eric B
The battles for Cassino *(London: Ian Allan 1975), 192p., bib.*

CAUSES [see ORIGINS]

CAVALRY

PIEKALKIEWICZ, Janusz
The cavalry of World War II *(London: Orbis 1979), 256p.*

CEYLON

TOMLINSON, Michael
The most dangerous moment *(London: Kimber 1976), 205p., bib.*

CHANNEL ISLANDS

ANTILL, J Kenneth
A bibliography of the German occupation of Jersey and other Channel Islands *(Jersey: States Greffe 1975), 31p.*

BONSOR, Noel R P
The Jersey Eastern Railway and the German occupation lines in Jersey *(Lingfield, Sy: Oakwood 1965), 142p.*

CHANNEL Islands occupation review *(Channel Islands Occupation Society 1975), 76p.*

CRUICKSHANK, Charles G
The German occupation of the Channel Islands *(London: OUP 1979), 370p.*

GINNS, Michael *and* BRYANS, Peter
The German fortifications in Jersey *(Grouville, Jersey: Ginns 1975), 93p., bib.*

HARRIS, Roger E
Islanders deported *(Ilford, Essex: CISS 1980), 226p., bib.*

HIGGS, Dorothy P
Guernsey diary 1940–1945: life in Guernsey under the Nazis *(St Peter Port, Guernsey: Toucan 1979), 65p.*

HOLMES, Denis C
Fortress Jersey *(Grouville, Jersey: Holmes 1978), 3 parts*

MARSHALL, M
  Hitler invaded Sark *(Guernsey: Paramount 1963)*, *60p.*

PACKE, M St J *and* DREYFUS, M
  The Alderney story, 1939—1949 *(Alderney: Alderney Society 1971)*, *152p.*

RAMSEY, Winston G
  The war in the Channel Islands then and now *(London: After the Battle 1981)*, *253p.*

STROOBANT, Frank W
  One man's war *(Guernsey: Guernsey Press 1967)*, *176p.*

TOMS, Carel
  Hitler's fortress islands *(London: New English Library 1978)*, *160p.*

TREMAYNE, Julia
  War on Sark: the secret letters of Julia Tremayne *(Exeter, Devon: Webb & Bower 1981)*, *208p.*

CHAPLAINS

DOW, A C
  A padre's parables *(Greenock, Scot: Orr: Pollock 1980)*, *75p.*

DUGGAN, Margaret *ed.*
  Padre in Colditz: the diary of J. Ellison Platt *(London: Hodder & Stoughton 1978)*, *319p.*

CHILDREN

BREED, Bryan
  I know a rotten place *(London: Arlington 1975)*, *117p.*

MASSEY, Victoria
  One child's war *(New York: Pubis 1978)*, *126p.*

MENEN, Aubrey
  Four days of Naples *(New York: Playboy 1979)*, *287p.*

SOSNOWSKI, Kiryl
The tragedy of children under Nazi rule *(New York: Fertig 1983), 381p.*

CHINA

BREWER, James F *and others eds.*
China airlift: the hump, China's aerial lifeline *(Poplar Bluff, Mo: Hump Pilots Association 1980), 596p.*

CORNELIUS, Wanda *and* SHORT, T A
Ding hao: America's air war in China, 1937—1945 *(London: Pelican 1980), unp.*

HEFLEY, James C *and* HEFLEY, M
The secret file on John Birch *(New York: Tyndale House 1980), 231p.*

MOSER, Don
China, Burma, India *(Alexandria, Va: Time-Life 1978), 208p.*

SCHALLER, Michael
The U.S. crusade in China, 1938—1945 *(Irvington, NY: Columbia UP), 364p.*

WILSON, Dick
When tigers fight: the story of the Sino-Japanese war, 1937—1945 *(London: Hutchinson 1982), 268p., bib.*

CHINDITS

BIDWELL, Shelford
The Chindit war: the campaign in Burma 1944 *(London: Hodder & Stoughton 1979), 304p., bib.*

JAMES, Richard J
Chindit *(London: Murray 1980), 214p., bib.*

[*see also BURMA*]

CHRONOLOGIES

CHRONOLOGY of the Second World War *(London: RIIA 1947), 446p. Later published as:* Chronology and Index of . . .

ROHWER, Jurgen *and* HUMMELCHEN, G
Chronology of the war at sea *(London: Allen 1972—74), 2 vols.*

SALMAGGI, Cesare *and* PALLAVASINI, A *comps*
2194 days of war: an illustrated chronology of the Second World War *(London: Windward 1979), 754p.*

CHURCHILL

GILBERT, Martin
Finest hour: Winston S. Churchill, 1939—1941 *(London: Heinemann 1983), 1308p.*

KERSAUDY, Francois
Churchill and De Gaulle *(London: Collins 1981), 476p., bib.*

LEWIN, R
Churchill as war lord *(London: Batsford 1973), 283p., bib.*

LOEWENHEIM, Francis W *and others*
Roosevelt and Churchill: their secret wartime correspondence *(New York: Saturday Review 1975), 805p.*

MOORE, R J
Churchill, Cripps and India, 1934—1945 *(London: OUP 1979), 162p.*

PELLING, H
Winston Churchill *(London: Macmillan 1974), 724p., bib.*

PITT, Barrie
Churchill and the Generals *(London: Sidgwick & Jackson 1981), 196p.*

ROSKILL, Stephen
Churchill and the Admirals *(London: Collins 1977), 351p.*

THOMPSON, R W
Churchill and Morton *(London: Hodder & Stoughton 1976), 223p.*

COASTAL COMMAND

BOWYER, Chaz
Coastal Command at war *(London: Ian Allan 1979), 160p., bib.*

COASTGUARDS

HORTON, Dick G
Fire over the islands: the coast watchers of the Solomons *(London: Cooper 1975), 256p.*

LORD, Walter
Lonely vigil: coastwatchers of the Solomons *(New York: Viking 1977), 322p.*

SCHEINA, Robert L
US Coastguard cutters and craft of World War II *(London: Naval Institute 1983), 384p.*

CODES AND CIPHERS

CLAYTON, Aileen
The enemy is listening *(London: Hutchinson 1980), 381p.*

HALDANE, R A
The hidden war *(London: Hale 1977), 208p.*

HOMEWOOD, Harry
Final harbor *(New York: McGraw-Hill 1980), 372p.*

KAHN, David
The code breakers *(New York: Macmillan 1967), 1164p., bib.*

RUSSELL, Francis
The secret war *(Alexandria, Va: Time-Life 1982), 208p.*
[*see also ENIGMA, MAGIC, PURPLE, ULTRA*]

COLLABORATORS

GORDON, Bertram M
Collaborationism in France during the Second World War
(London: Orbis 1980), 393p., bib.

LA MAZIERE, Christian de
Ashes of honour *(London: Wingate 1975), 319p.*

RINGS, Werner
Life with the enemy: collaboration and resistance in
Hitler's Europe, 1939—1945 *(New York: Doubleday
1982), 351p.*

COMMANDERS (general)

BLAXLAND, Gregory
Alexander's Generals: the Italian campaign, 1944—45
(London: Kimber 1979), 320p.

TAYLOR, A J P
The war lords *(London: Hamilton 1977), 189p.*

COMMANDOS

BUTLER, Rupert
Hands of steel: the story of the Commandos *(London:
Hamlyn 1980), 261p.*

FOXHALL, Raymond
The amateur commandos *(London: Hale 1980), 159p.*

GILCHRIST, Donald
Don't cry for me: the Commandos, D-Day and after
(London: Hale 1982), 192p.

HAMPSHIRE, A Cecil
The beachhead Commandos *(London: Kimber 1983),* *208p., bib.*

INFIELD, Glenn B
Skorzeny: Hitler's commando *(New York: St Martin's* *1981), 266p.*

LADD, James D
Commandos and the Rangers of World War II *(London:* *St Martin's 1978), 288p.*

STOKES, E G
Lower the ramps: experiences with the 43rd Royal
Marines Commando in Yugoslavia *(Maidstone, Kent:* *Mann 1974), 136p.*

YOUNG, Desmond
Fourfive: the story of 45 Commando, Royal Marines,
1943−1971 *(London: Cooper 1972), 463p.*

[*see also ROYAL MARINES, US RANGERS*]

CONCENTRATION CAMPS

AINZSTEIN, Reuben
The Sobibor uprising: Jewish resistance in Nazi-occupied
Eastern Europe *(London: Elek 1974), 992p.*

BERBEN, Paul
Dachau, 1933−1945 *(London: Norfolk 1975), 300p., bib.*

DES PRES, Terrence
The survivor: an anatomy of life in the death camps *(New* *York: OUP 1976), 218p.*

DONAT, Alexander *ed.*
The death camp Treblinka *(New York: Holocaust 1979),* *320p.*

GARLINSKI, Jozef
Fighting Auschwitz: the resistance movement in the concentration camp *(London: Friedman 1975), 319p.*

GILBERT, Martin
Auschwitz and the Allies: how the Allies responded to the news of Hitler's final solution *(London: Joseph 1981), 368p.*

HART, Kitty
Return to Auschwitz: the remarkable story of a girl who survived the holocaust *(London: Sidgwick & Jackson 1981), 178p.*

KIELAR, Wieslaw
Anus mundi: 1500 days in Auschwitz/Birkenau *(New York: Times 1980), 312p.*

LEVY-HASS, Hanna
Inside Belsen *(Brighton, Sx: Harvester 1982), 134p.*

MICHEL, Jan *and* NUCERA, L
Dora *(London: Weidenfeld & Nicolson 1979), 308p.*

MULLER, Filip
Auschwitz inferno: the testimony of a Sonder kommando *(London: Routledge & Kegan Paul 1979), 180p.*
US title: Eyewitness Auschwitz

NOVITCH, Miriam
Sobibor: martyrdom and revolt *(New York: Holocaust 1980)*

PAWELCZYASKA, Anna
Values and violence in Auschwitz: a sociological analysis *(London: University of California 1979), 170p.*

PISAR, Samuel
Of blood and hope *(London: Cassell 1980), 320p.*

RASHKE, Richard
Escape from Sobibor *(London: Joseph 1983), 389p.*

RASSINIER, Paul
Debunking the genocide myth: a study of the Nazi concentration camps and the alleged extermination of European Jews *(Los Angeles, Cal: Noontide 1978), 441p.*

RICHMAN, Leon
Why?: extermination camp Lwow (Lemberg) 134 Janowska Street, Poland *(New York: Vantage 1975), 273p.*

ROCHMAN, Leyb
The pit and the trap: a chronicle of survival *(New York: Holocaust 1983), 271p.*

SELZER, Michael
Deliverance day: the last hours at Dachau *(Philadelphia, Pa: Lippincott 1978), 250p., bib.*

SERENY, Gitta
Into that darkness: from mercy killing to mass murder *(London: Deutsch 1976), 380p.*

STEINER, Jean F
Treblinka *(New York: New American Library 1979), 304p.*

TEN BOOM, Corrie
Corrie Ten Boom's prison letters *(New York: Revell 1975), 90p.*
The hiding place *(London: Hodder & Stoughton 1972), 221p.*

TILLION, Germaine
Ravensbruck *(New York: Doubleday 1975), 256p.*

[*see also GERMANY, GESTAPO, JEWS, POLAND*]

CONSCIENTIOUS OBJECTORS

BARKER, Rachel
Conscience, government and war: conscientious objection in Great Britain, 1939—45 *(London: Routledge & Kegan Paul 1982), 174p., bib.*

PARTRIDGE, Frances
A pacifist's war *(London: Hogarth 1978), 223p.*

SPRING, Ernest C T
Conchie: the wartime experiences of a conscientious objector *(London: Cooper 1975), 122p.*

ZAHN, Gordon C
Another part of the war: conscientious objector: the Camp
Simon story *(Amherst, Mass: University of Massachusetts
1979), 273p.*

CONVOYS

ELLIOTT, Peter
Allied escort ships of World War II: a complete survey
(London: Macdonald & Jane's 1977), 575p.

KEMP, Peter K
Decision at sea: the convoy escort *(New York: Dutton
1978), 184p.*

MIDDLEBROOK, Martin
Convoy: the battles for convoys SC.122 and HX.229
(London: Ian Allan 1976), 378p., bib.

MOORE, W J
Diaries and memoirs of a sailor *(Ilfracombe, Devon:
Stockwell 1983), 76p.*

PEARCE, Frank
Last call for HMS Edinburgh: a story of the Russian convoys *(London: Collins 1982), 202p., bib.*

REVELY, Henry
The convoy that nearly died: the story of ONS 154
(London: Kimber 1979), 222p., bib.

ROHWER, Jurgen
The critical convoy battles of March 1943: the battle for
HX.229, SC.122 *(London: Ian Allan 1977), 256p., bib.*

SCHOFIELD, Brian B
The Arctic convoys *(London: Macdonald & Jane's 1977),
198p., bib.*

SMITH, Peter C
Arctic victory: the story of Convoy PQ 18 *(London:
Kimber 1975), 238p.*

[*see also MERCHANT NAVY, ROYAL NAVY, U-BOATS*]

CORAL SEA

HOYT, Edwin P
Blue skies and blood: the battle of Coral Sea *(New York: Pinnacle 1976), 258p.*

CORREGIDOR

BELOTE, James H *and* BELOTE, W M
Corregidor *(New York: Playboy 1980), 270p.*

MORRIS, Eric
Corregidor *(London: Hutchinson 1982), 512p.*

[*see also BATAAN, PACIFIC, PHILIPPINES*]

COVENTRY

LONGMATE, Norman
Air raid: the bombing of Coventry, 1940 *(London: Hutchinson 1976), 302p., bib.*

CRETE

FEATHERSTONE, Donald F
Wargaming airborne operations *(Cranbury, NJ: Barnes 1979), 250p.*

SIMPSON, Tony
Operation Mercury: the battle for Crete, 1941 *(London: Hodder & Stoughton 1981), 316p., bib.*

THOMAS, David A
Crete 1941: the battle at sea *(London: New English Library 1976), 224p.*

CRUISERS

CONNELL, G G
  Valiant quartet: His Majesty's anti-aircraft cruisers 'Curlew', 'Cairo', 'Calcutta', and 'Coventry' *(London: Kimber 1979), 303p.*

HAINES, Gregory
  Cruiser at war *(London: Ian Allan 1978), 144p.*

MONTGOMERY, Michael
  Who sank the Sydney? *(London: Cooper & Secker & Warburg 1983)*

PARGETER, C J
  "Hipper" class heavy cruisers *(London: Ian Allan 1982), 80p.*

PEARCE, Frank
  Last call for HMS Edinburgh *(London: Collins 1982), 202p., bib.*
  The ship that torpedoed herself (HMS Trinidad) *(Plymouth, Devon: Bacon Jay 1975), 181p.*

SMITH, Peter C *and* DOMINY, John R
  Cruisers in action, 1939—1945 *(London: Kimber 1981), 320p.*

  [*see also GERMAN NAVY, ROYAL NAVY, US NAVY*]

DAKAR

MARDER, Arthur J
  Operation menace: the Dakar expedition and the Dudley North affair *(London: OUP 1976), 289p.*

PLIMMER, Charlotte *and* PLIMMER, Denis
  A matter of expediency: the jettison of Admiral Sir Dudley North *(London: Quartet 1978), 156p., bib.*

WILLIAMS, John
  The guns of Dakar *(London: Heinemann 1976), 201p., bib.*

D-DAY

GOLLEY, John
The big drop: the guns of Merville, June 1944 *(London: Jane's 1982), 174p., bib.*

HASWELL, Jock
The intelligence and deception of the D-Day landings *(London: Batsford 1979), 208p., bib.*
US title: D-Day

MARRIN, Albert
Overlord: D-Day and the invasion of Europe *(New York: Atheneum 1982), 177p.*

PAINE, L D
D-Day *(London: Hale 1981), 192p.*

WARNER, Philip
The D-Day landings *(London: Kimber 1980), 309p.*

[*see also* NORMANDY]

DECORATIONS AND MEDALS

FEVYER, W H
The Distinguished Service Medal, 1939–1946 *(London: London Stamp Exchange 1981), 163p.*
The George Medal, 1940–1945 *(London: Spink 1980), 114p.*

GROSVENOR, Gilbert
Insignia and decorations of the U.S. Armed Forces *(Washington DC: National Geographical Society 1945), 208p.*

[*see also* VICTORIA CROSS]

DENMARK

THOMAS, John O
The giant-killers: the story of the Danish resistance movement, 1940—1945 *(London: Joseph 1975), 320p.*

DEPORTATION

GARDINER, Clinton H
Pawns in a triangle of hate: the Peruvian-Japanese and the United States *(Seattle: University of Washington 1981), 222p.*

DESTROYERS

CONNELL, G G
Fighting destroyer: the story of HMS Petard *(London: Kimber 1976), 271p., bib.*

FERNALD, J
Destroyer from America *(London: Cape 1942), 127p.*

GRIGGS, G P
Destroyer at war *(London: Hutchinson 1942), 128p.*

HAINES, Gregory
Destroyers at war *(London: Ian Allan 1982), 128p.*

HILL, Roger
Destroyer captain *(London: Kimber 1975), 255p.*

MACK, George
HMS Intrepid: a memoir *(London: Kimber 1980), 208p., bib.*

REILLY, John C *jun.*
United States Navy destroyers of World War II *(Poole, Dorset: Blandford 1983), 163p.*

SMITH, Peter C
Fighting flotilla: HMS Laforey and her sister ships *(London: Kimber 1976), 224p.*

WHITLEY, M J
German destroyers in World War II *(London: Arms & Armour 1983), 300p.*

WINTON, John
Sink the Haguro!: the last destroyer action of the Second World War *(London: Seeley Service & Cooper 1979), 182p.*

DIEPPE

ATKIN, Ronald
Dieppe 1942: the jubilee disaster *(London: Macmillan 1980), 306p., bib.*

FRANKS, Norman L R
The greatest air battle: Dieppe 19th August 1942 *(London: Kimber 1979), 256p.*

LEASOR, James
Green beach *(London: Heinemann 1975), 288p., bib.*

MELLOR, John
The forgotten heroes: the Canadians at Dieppe *(Toronto: Methuen 1975), 163p. Later published as:* Dunkirk

PROUSE, Robert A
Ticket to hell via Dieppe *(Exeter, Devon: Webb & Bower 1982), 208p.*

WHITEHEAD, W
Dieppe 1942: echoes of disaster *(Toronto: Personal Library 1979), 187p.*
Dieppe 1942 *(Glasgow: Drew 1982), 91p.*

DIPLOMATIC HISTORY

BARKER, Elizabeth
British policy in South-East Europe in the Second World War *(London: Macmillan 1976), 320p.*
Churchill and Eden at war *(London: Macmillan 1978), 346p., bib.*

BRYSON, Thomas A
Seeds of MidEast crisis: the United States diplomatic role in the Middle East during World War II *(Jefferson, NC: McFarland 1981), 216p.*

DARILEK, Richard E
A loyal opposition in time of war: the Republican Party and the politics of foreign policy from Pearl Harbor to Yalta *(Westport, Conn: Greenwood 1976), 239p.*

DAVIS, Lynn E
The cold war begins: Soviet-American conflict over Eastern Europe *(Princeton, NJ: Princeton UP 1974), 427p.*

DOUGLAS, Roy
New alliances *(New York: St Martin's 1981), 224p.*

EISENHOWER, John S D
Allies: Pearl Harbor to D-Day *(New York: Doubleday 1982), 500p.*

FODOR, Denis J
The neutrals *(Alexandria, Va: Time-Life 1982), 208p.*

GATES, Eleanor M
End of the affair: the collapse of the Anglo-French alliance, 1939—1940 *(Berkeley, Cal: University of California 1981), 630p.*

HARRIMAN, William A
Special envoy to Churchill and Stalin, 1941—1946 *(New York: Random House 1975), 595p.*

HERWARTH von BITTENFELD, H *and* STARR, S
Against two evils *(New York: Rawson-Wade 1981), 318p.*

KACAWICZ, George V
Great Britain, the Soviet Union and the Polish Government in exile, 1934—1945 *(Hague, Neth: Nijhoff 1979), 255p.*

LAUNAY, Jacques de
Secret diplomacy of World War II *(New York: Simmons-Boardman 1963), 175p.*

LOUIS, William R
Imperialism at bay: the U.S. and the decolonisation of the British Empire, 1941—1945 *(New York: OUP 1978), 594p.*

LUKAS, Richard C
The strange allies: the United States and Poland, 1941—1945 *(Knoxville, Tenn: University of Tennessee 1978), 230p.*

McSHERRY, James E
Stalin, Hitler and Europe *(Arlington, Va: Open-door 1977), 2 vols.*

NEWMAN, Simon
March 1939: the British guarantee to Poland *(Oxford: Clarendon 1976), 253p., bib.*

NOWAK, Jan
Courier from Warsaw *(Detroit, Mich: Wayne State UP 1982), 477p.*

ROSE, Lisle A
The long shadow: reflections on the Second World War *(Westport, Conn: Greenwood 1978), 224p.*

SMITH, Bradley F *and* AGARESSI, E
Operation sunrise: the secret surrender *(London: Deutsch 1979), 234p.*

TAUBMAN, William
Stalin's American policy: from entente to detente to cold war *(New York: Norton 1982), 291p.*

THORNE, Christopher G
Allies of a kind: the United States, Britain and the war against Japan, 1941—1945 *(London: Hamilton 1978), 772p.*

WEBER, Frank G
The evasive neutral: Germany, Britain and the quest of the Turkish alliance in the Second World War *(Columbia, Mo: University of Missouri Press 1979), 244p.*

WOODWARD, *Sir* Llewellyn
British foreign policy in the Second World War *(London: HMSO 1962−1976), 5 vols.*

DRESDEN

McKEE, Alex
Dresden: the devil's tinderbox *(London: Souvenir 1982), 332p., bib.*

DUNKIRK

BARKER, Arthur J
Dunkirk: the great escape *(London: Dent 1977), 240p., bib.*

CHATTERTON, E K
The epic of Dunkirk *(London: Hurst & Blackett 1940), 256p.*

FRANKS, Norman L R
The air battle of Dunkirk *(London: Kimber 1983), 236p.*

GROSSMITH, Frederick
Dunkirk − a miracle of deliverance *(London: Bachman & Turner 1978), 120p.*

HARMAN, Nicholas
Dunkirk: the necessary myth *(London: Hodder & Stoughton 1980), 271p., bib.*

HARRIS, John
Dunkirk: the storms of war *(Newton Abbot, Devon: David & Charles 1980), 160p.*

JACKSON, Robert
Dunkirk: the British evacuation, 1940 *(London: Barker 1976), 206p., bib.*

LORD, Walter
The miracle of Dunkirk *(New York: Viking 1982), 323p.*

TURNBULL, Patrick
Dunkirk: anatomy of a miracle *(London: Batsford 1978), 186p.*

EAST AFRICA

CROSSKILL, W E
The two thousand mile war *(London: Hale 1980), 224p., bib.*

EASTERN EUROPE

ABBOTT, Peter *and* THOMAS, Nigel
Germany's Eastern Front allies, 1941—45 *(London: Osprey 1982), 40p.*

COOPER, Matthew
The phantom war: the German struggle against Soviet partisans, 1941—1944 *(London: Macdonald & Jane's 1978), 216p.*
US title: The Nazi war against Soviet partisans

DUPUY, Trevor N *and* MARTELL, Paul
Great battles on the Eastern Front: the Soviet—German war, 1941—1945 *(Minneapolis: Bobbs-Merrill 1982), 249p.*

LUCAS, James
War on the Eastern Front, 1941—1945: the German soldier in Russia *(London: Jane's 1979), 214p., bib.*

QUARRIE, Bruce *comp.*
Waffen SS in Russia: a selection of German wartime photos *(Cambridge: Stephens 1978), 95p.*

THE RUSSIAN FRONT *(London: Arms & Armour 1978), 200p.*

SHTEMENKO, S M
The last six months: the first authentic account of Russia's final battles with Hitler's Armies in World War II *(London: Kimber 1978), 436p.*

TAYLOR, A J P
The Russian war, 1941—1945 *(London: Cape 1978), 143p.*

WAR in the East: the Russo—German conflict, 1941—45 *(New York: Hippocrene 1977), 186p.*

ZALOGA, Steven J *and* GRANDSEN, James
The Eastern Front: armour camouflage and markings, 1941 to 1945 *(London: Arms & Armour 1983), 96p., bib.*

ZHILIN, P
They sealed their own doom *(Moscow: Progress 1970), 262p.*

ZIEMKE, Earl F
Stalingrad to Berlin: the German defeat in the East *(Washington DC: Dept of the Army 1968), 549p.*

E BOATS

BEAVER, Paul *comp.*
E-boats and coastal craft *(Cambridge: Stephens 1980), 94p.*

COOPER, Bryan
The E-boat threat *(London: Macdonald & Jane's 1976), 138p., bib.*

ECONOMICS

DOUGHERTY, James J
The politics of war time aid: American economic assistance to France and French North-West Africa, 1940—1946 *(London: Greenwood 1978), 264p., bib.*

DRAPER, Albert
Operation Fish: the race to save Europe's wealth, 1939—1945 *(London: Cassell 1979), 377p., bib.*

MILWARD, Alan S
War, economy and society, 1939—1945 *(London: Lane 1977), 395p., bib.*

SOUTHARD, Frank A
The finances of European liberation with special reference to Italy *(New York: Arno 1979), 206p.*

EICHMANN

HAREL, Isser
The house on Garibaldi Street: the capture of Adolf Eichmann *(London: Deutsch 1975), 316p.*

EISENHOWER

EISENHOWER, Dwight D
The papers of Dwight David Eisenhower *(Baltimore: Johns-Hopkins UP 1973), 9 vols.*

FERRELL, R.H. *ed.*
The Eisenhower diaries *(New York: Norton 1981), 445p.*

EL ALAMEIN

DOUGLAS, Keith C
Alamein to Zem Zem *(London: OUP 1979), 156p.*

LUCAS, James
War in the desert: the Eighth Army at El Alamein *(London: Arms & Armour 1982), 283p., bib.*

MAUGHAM, Barton
Tobruk and El Alamein *(Canberra, Aust: Australian War Memorial 1974), 854p.*

PITT, Barrie
The crucible of war: year of Alamein *(London: Cape 1982), 478p.*

STRAWSON, John
El Alamein desert victory *(London: Dent 1981), 191p., bib.*

WARNER, Philip
Alamein *(London: Kimber 1979), 239p.*

*[see also BRITISH ARMY (EIGHTH ARMY),
MONTGOMERY, NORTH AFRICA, ROMMEL]*

ENCYCLOPAEDIAS

BAUDOT, Marcel *ed.*
The historical encyclopaedia of World War II *(London: Macmillan 1981), 548p.*

THE ENCYCLOPAEDIA of World War II *(London: Secker & Warburg 1978), 787p.*

GUNSTON, Bill
The illustrated encyclopaedia of combat aircraft of World War II *(London: Salamander 1978), 261p.*

HOGG, Ian V
The encyclopaedia of infantry weapons of World War II *(London: Arms & Armour 1977), 192p.*

MARSHALL CAVENDISH encyclopaedia of World War II *(London: Marshall Cavendish 1981), 11 vols.*

PARISH, Thomas D *ed.*
The Simon & Schuster encyclopaedia of World War II *(New York: Simon & Schuster 1978), 761p.*

THE RAND-McNALLY encyclopaedia of World War II *(London: Bison 1977), 256p.*

SNYDER, Louis L
Encyclopaedia of the Third Reich *(London: Hale 1976), 410p., bib.*

YOUNG, Peter *ed.*
The Almanac of World War II *(London: Hamlyn, nd), 613p.*

ENIGMA

GARLINSKI, Jozef
Intercept: the enigma war *(London: Dent 1979), 213p.*
US title: The enigma war

WELCHMAN, Gordon
The hut six story: breaking the Enigma codes *(New York: McGraw-Hill 1982), 326p.*

[*see also CODES AND CIPHERS, ULTRA*]

ENTERTAINMENT

FAWKES, Richard
Fighting for a laugh: entertaining the British and American Armed Forces, 1939–1945 *(London: Macdonald & Jane's 1978), 192p.*

HUGGETT, Frank
Goodnight sweetheart: songs and memories of the Second World War *(London: W.H. Allen 1979), 192p.*

HUGHES, John G
The greasepaint war: show business, 1939–45 *(London: New English Library 1976), 216p.*

LEITCH, Michael *ed.*
Great songs of World War II; with the Home Front in pictures *(London: Wise 1975), 181p.*

ESCAPES

BISHOP, Jack
In pursuit of freedom *(London: Cooper 1977), 126p.*

BOSANQUET, David
Escape through China *(London: Hale 1983), 261p.*

BRADLEY, James
Towards the setting sun: an escape from the Thailand–Burma railway, 1943 *(London: Phillimore 1982), 139p.*

DARLING, Donald
Secret Sunday *(London: Kimber 1975), 208p.*

FOOT, M R D *and* LANGLEY, J M
MI9: escape and evasion, 1939–1945 *(London: Bodley Head 1979), 365p.*

GARIOCH, Robert
Two men and a blanket: memoirs of escapes *(Edinburgh: Southside 1975), 183p.*

GRAHAM, Burton
Escape from the swastika *(London: Marshall Cavendish 1975), 120p.*

GRIFFITHS, Frank
Winged hours *(London: Kimber 1981), 192p.*

HACKETT, *Sir* John
I was a stranger *(London: Chatto & Windus 1977), 219p.*

HANSON, S E
Underground out of Holland *(London: Ian Allan 1977), 191p.*

JAMES, B A
Moonless night *(London: Kimber 1983)*

JONES, Donald I
Escape from Sulmona *(New York: Vantage 1980), 147p.*

KESSEL, Lipmann
Surgeon at arms *(London: Heinemann 1958)*

LANGLEY, James M
Fight another day *(London: Collins 1974), 245p.*

MARLOW, Roy
Beyond the wire *(London: Hale 1983), 192p.*

MOORE, John H
The faustball tunnel: German POW's in America and their great escape *(New York: Random House 1978), 268p.*

NEWMAN, Philip
Safer than a known way: an escape story of World War II *(London: Kimber 1983)*

ORNA, Joseph
The escaping habit *(London: Cooper 1975), 143p.*

TREBICH, Willy
The broken swastika *(London: Cooper 1973), 184p.*

WILLIAMS, Elvet
Arbeits-kommando *(London: Gollancz 1975), 256p.*

WOODS, Rex
Night train to Innsbruck: a commando's escape to freedom *(London: Kimber 1983)*

[*see also PRISONERS-OF-WAR*]

ESPIONAGE [see INTELLIGENCE, SECRET SERVICE]

EVACUEES

BAILEY, Anthony
America, lost and found *(New York: Random House 1981), 152p.*

GRUNFELD, Judith
Shelford: the story of a Jewish school community in evacuation, 1939—1945 *(London: Soncino 1980), 125p.*

MACLEAN, Meta
The singing ship: an odyssey of evacuee children *(Bath: Chivers 1975), 256p.*

FALAISE GAP

LUCAS, James S *and* BARKER, A J
The killing ground: the battle of the Falaise Gap, August 1944 *(London: Batsford 1978), 176p.*
US title: The battle of Normandy

ROHMER, Richard
Patton's gap: an account of the battle of Normandy, 1944
(London: Arms & Armour 1981), 240p., bib.

[*see also NORMANDY, PATTON, WESTERN EUROPE
1944—45*]

FAR EAST

ALLEN Louis
The end of the war in Asia *(London: Hart-Davis,
MacGibbon 1976), 306p., bib.*

COLLIER, Basil
Japan at war: an illustrated history of the war in the Far
East, 1931—1945 *(London: Sidgwick & Jackson 1975),
192p.*

FIGHTERS

ALLEN, Hubert P
Fighter squadron: a memoir, 1940—1942 *(London:
Kimber 1979), 192p.*

ALLWARD, Maurice
Hurricane special *(London: Ian Allan 1975), 64p.*

BADER, Douglas *comp.*
Fight for the sky: the story of the Spitfire and the
Hurricane *(London: Sidgwick & Jackson 1975), 168p.*

BARCLAY, George
Fighter pilot *(London: Kimber 1976), 224p. Later published as:* Angels 22

BARKER, Ralph
The Hurricane *(London: Pelham 1978), 207p.*

BLEDSOE, Marvin V
Thunderbolt: memoirs of a World War II fighter pilot
(New York: Van Nostrand 1982), 282p.

BOWYER, Chaz
  Beaufighter at war *(London: Ian Allan 1976), 160p., bib.*
  Hurricane at war *(London: Ian Allan 1974), 160p.*
  Spitfire *(London: Arms & Armour 1980), 64p.*
  Supermarine Spitfire *(London: Arms & Armour 1980), 64p.*

BROOKES, Andrew J *comp.*
  Fighter squadron at war *(London: Ian Allan 1980), 144p.*

CAIN, Charles W *and* JERRAM, M
  Fighters of World War II *(Windsor, Berks: Profile 1979), 128p.*

CHRISTIE, Joe
  P-40 Hawks at war *(London: Ian Allan 1979), 128p.*

CHRISTIE, Joe *and* ETHELL, J L
  P-38 Lightning at war *(London: Ian Allan 1978), 144p.*

DONNET, Mike
  Flight to freedom *(London: Ian Allan 1974), 108p.*

DUNN, William R
  Fighter pilot: the first American ace of World War II *(Lexington, Kty: University of Kentucky 1982), 234p.*

FRANCILLON, Rene J
  USAAF fighter units: Europe, 1942—45 *(London: Osprey 1977), 48p.*

FRANKS, Norman L R
  Fighter leader: the story of Wing Commander Ian Gleed *(London: Kimber 1978), 207p.*

FREEMAN, Roger A
  Thunderbolt: a documentary history of the Republic P-47 *(London: Macdonald & Jane's 1978), 152p.*

GRANT, Bill N
  P-51 Mustang *(London: Arms & Armour 1980), 64p.*

GUNSTON, Bill
  An illustrated guide to German, Italian and Japanese fighters of World War II *(New York: Arco 1980), 159p.*
  Night fighters: a development and combat history *(Cambridge: Stephens 1976), 192p.*

GUTHRIE, David *ed.*
Spitfire squadron *(London: Hale 1978), 160p.*

GUYS, Wladek
First kill: a fighter pilot's autobiography *(London: Kimber 1981), 207p.*

HALL, Alan W
American fighters of World War II *(Cambridge: Stephens 1976), 64p.*

HALL, Grover C
1000 destroyed: the life and times of the 4th Fighter Group *(Fallbrook, Cal: Aero 1978), 384p.*

HALLEY, J J
Famous fighter squadrons of the RAF *(Windsor, Berks: Profile 1971), vol.I*

ILFREY, Jack *and* REYNOLDS, Max
Happy Jack's go-buggy: a World War II fighter pilot's personal document *(Hicksville, NY: Exposition 1979), 167p.*

JACKSON, Robert
Fighter pilots of World War II *(London: Barker 1976), 176p.*
Fighter!: the story of air combat, 1936—45 *(London: Barker 1979), 168p.*

McDOWELL, Ernest R
P-39 Airacobra in action *(Carrolton, Tex: Squadron Signal 1980), 46p.*

MASON, Francis K
British fighters of World War Two *(Windsor, Berks: Lacy 1970), 64p.*

NESS, William N
Thunderbolt at war *(London: Ian Allan 1976), 160p.*

PAGE, Geoffrey
Tale of a guinea pig *(London: Pelham 1981), 218p.*

PHILPOTT, Bryan
RAF fighter units, Europe, 1939–1942 *(London: Osprey 1977), 48p.*
RAF combat units, SEAC, 1941–45 *(London: Osprey 1979), 48p.*

PRICE, Alfred
Spitfire: a documentary history *(London: Macdonald & Jane's 1977), 159p.*
Spitfire at war *(London: Ian Allan 1974), 160p.*
World War II fighter conflict *(London: Macdonald & Jane's 1975), 160p., bib.*

QUILL, Jeffrey
Spitfire: a test pilot's story *(London: Murray 1983), 316p.*

RAWLINGS, J D R
Fighter squdrons of the RAF and their aircraft *(London: Macdonald & Jane's 1976), rev. ed. 572p.*

REVELL, Alex
The vivid air: Gerald and Michael Constable Maxwell, fighter pilots in both World Wars *(London: Kimber 1978), 255p.*

RICHEY, Paul
Fighter pilot: a personal record of the campaign in France, 1939–1940 *(London: Macdonald & Jane's 1980), 142p.*

SCOTT, Desmond
Typhoon pilot *(London: Secker & Warburg 1982), 168p.*

SHORES, Christopher *and others*
Fighters over Tunisia *(London: Spearman 1975), 491p.*

SMITH, W G G
Spitfire into battle *(London: Murray 1981), 235p.*

SMITHERS, Alan J
Wonder aces of the air *(London: Gordon & Cremonesi 1979), 192p.*

STAFFORD, Gene B
Aces of the South West Pacific *(Carrolton, Tex: Squadron Signal 1977), 64p.*

STEWART, Adrian
  Hurricane: the war exploits of the fighter aircraft *(London: Kimber 1982), 336p.*

STOKES, Doug
  Paddy Finucane: fighter ace *(London: Kimber 1983), 219p.*

SULLIVAN, Jim
  F4U Corsair in action *(Carrolton, Tex: Squadron Signal 1977), 49p.*

TILLMAN, Barrett
  Hellcat: the F6F in World War II *(Cambridge: Stephens 1979), 365p.*
  Corsair: the F4U in World War II and Korea *(Annapolis, Md: Naval Institute 1979), 219p.*

TURNER, John F
  The Bader wing *(London: Midas 1981), 153p.*

WEAL, Elke C *and others*
  Combat aircraft of World War II *(London: Arms & Armour 1977), 238p.*

WHITE, Roger H
  Spitfire saga: with a spell in Wellingtons *(London: Kimber 1981), 221p.*

WYKEHAM, Peter
  Fighter Command *(New York: Arno 1980), 320p.*

FILMS

MORELLA, Joe *and others*
  Films of World War II *(Secaurus, NJ: Citadel 1973), 256p.*

THORPE, Frances *and others*
  British official films in the Second World War: a descriptive catalogue *(London: Clio 1980), 321p.*

FINANCE

HIGHAM, Charles
Trading with the enemy: an expose of the Nazi—American money plot, 1933—1949 *(New York: Delacorte 1983)*, *277p.*

FINLAND

ELTING, John R
Battles for Scandinavia *(Alexandria, Va: Time-Life 1981)*, *208p.*

LUUKKANEN, Eino A
Fighter over Finland *(New York: Arno 1980)*, *254p.*

FIREFIGHTERS

WALLINGTON, Neil
Firemen at war: the work of London's firefighters in the 2nd World War *(Newton Abbot, Devon: David & Charles 1981)*, *222p., bib.*

FLEET AIR ARM

HOARE, John
Tumult in the clouds: a story of the Fleet Air Arm *(London: Joseph 1976)*, *208p.*

KILBRACKEN, John G *baron*
Bring back my stringbag: Swordfish pilot at war *(London: Davies 1979)*, *227p.*

LAMB, Charles
War in a stringbag *(London: Cassell 1977)*, *340p.*

WINTON, John
Find, fix and strike: the Fleet Air Arm at war, 1939—45 *(London: Batsford 1980)*, *152p.*

FLYING BOATS

BOWYER, Chaz
Sunderland at war *(London: Ian Allan 1976), 160p.*

FLYING BOMBS

COOKSLEY, Peter G
Flying bomb *(London: Hale 1979), 208p.*

JOHNSON, David
V for vengeance: the second battle of London *(London: Kimber 1981), 203p.*

LONGMATE, Norman
The doodlebugs: the story of the flying-bombs *(London: Hutchinson 1981), 549p., bib.*

YOUNG, Richard A
The flying bomb *(London: Ian Allan 1978), 160p., bib.*

[*see also SECRET WEAPONS*]

FOOD

GRANT, Ian *and* MADDREN, N
The countryside at war *(London: Jupiter 1975), 128p.*

FRANCE

ADAMTHWAITE, Anthony P
France and the coming of the Second World War, 1936—1939 *(London: Cass 1977), 434p., bib.*

BARBER, Noel
The week France fell: June 1940 *(London: Macmillan 1976), 320p., bib.*

CARLISLE, Olga
Island in time: a memoir of childhood *(New York: Rinehart 1980), 226p.*

COBB, Richard
French and Germans, Germans and French: a personal interpretation of France under two occupations, 1914—1918/1940—1944 *(Hanover, NH: University Press of New England 1983), 188p., bib.*

DANK, Milton
The French against the French: collaboration and resistance *(Philadelphia, Pa: Lippincott 1974), 365p., bib.*

DU CROS, Janet T
Divided loyalties *(London: Hamilton 1962), 330p.*

HUNT, Antonia
Little resistance: a teenage English girl's adventures in occupied France *(New York: St Martin's 1982), 149p.*

JARDIN, Pascal
Vichy boyhood: an inside view of the Petain regime *(London: Faber 1975), 136p.*

JOFFO, Joseph
A bag of marbles *(London: Joseph 1975), 208p.*

KEDWARD, Harry R
Resistance in Vichy France: a study of ideas and motivation in the southern zone, 1940—1942 *(London: OUP 1978), 311p., bib.*

PAPANEK, Ernst *and* LINN, Edward
Out of the fire *(New York: Morrow 1975), 299p.*

SPANIER, Ginette
Long road to freedom: the story of her life under German occupation *(London: Hale 1976), 172p.*

THOMAS, R T
Britain and Vichy: the dilemma of Anglo-French relations, 1940—42 *(London: Macmillan 1979), 230p., bib.*

[see also NORTH-WEST EUROPE 1939—1940, RESISTANCE]

FRENCH ARMY

GUNSBERG, Jeffery A
Divided and conquered: the French High Command and
the defeat of the West, 1940 *(Westport, Conn: Greenwood
1979), 398p.*

HORNE, Alistair
To lose a battle: France 1940 *(London: Penguin 1969),
704p.*

JACKSON, Robert
The fall of France: May—June 1940 *(London: Barker
1975), 189p., bib.*

FROGMEN

BLASSINGAME, Wyatt
Underwater warriors *(New York: Random House 1982),
151p. First published as:* The U.S. frogmen of World War
II

GERMANY

BRADLEY, John
The illustrated history of the Third Reich *(London: Bison
1978), 256p.*

CARGILL, Morris *ed.*
A gallery of Nazis *(Secausus, NJ: Stuart 1978), 224p.*

DOBSON, Christopher *and others*
The cruellest night: Germany's Dunkirk and the sinking of
the Wilhelm Gustoff *(London: Hodder & Stoughton
1979), 233p.*

FORSTER, Anneliese
Wooden monkeys *(Chicago, Mich: Academy Chicago
1979), 158p.*

FROMM, Erich
The anatomy of human destructiveness *(New York: Holt 1973), 521p.*
Escape from freedom *(New York: Holt 1941), 305p.*

GLEES, Anthony
Exile politics during the Second World War: the German Soviet democrat in Britain *(Oxford: Clarendon 1982), 340p.*

GOODENOUGH, Simon *ed.*
Hitler's war machine *(London: Hamlyn 1976), 248p., bib.*

GRUN, Max von der
Howl like the wolves: growing up in Nazi Germany *(New York: Morrow 1980), 285p.*

GRUNFELD, Frederic V
The Hitler file: a social history of Germany and the Nazis, 1918—45 *(London: Book Club Associates 1974), 374p.*

HARING, Bernhard
Embattled witness: memories of a time of war *(New York: Seabury 1976), 116p.*

HERZSTEIN, Robert E
The Nazis *(Alexandria, Va: Time-Life 1980), 208p.*

HILLGRUBER, Andreas
Germany and two world wars *(Cambridge, Mass: Harvard UP 1981), 120p.*

HOFFMAN, Peter
The history of the German resistance, 1933—1945 *(London: Macdonald & Jane's 1977), 864p.*

KOCH, H Wolfgang
The Hitler youth, origins and development, 1922—1945 *(London: Macdonald & Jane's 1975), 340p., bib.*

KRAUSNICK, H *and others*
Anatomy of the SS State *(London: Commins 1968), 614p., bib.*

LANG, Daniel
A backward look: Germans remember *(New York: McGraw-Hill 1979), 112p.*

MAYER, S L *ed.*
Hitler's wartime magazine 'Signal' *(London: Hamlyn 1976), 192p.*

MURNIEKE, Lise M
The way we lived in Germany during World War II: a personal account *(Scarborough, W.Aust: Arale 1977), 172p.*

REYNOLDS, Nicholas
Treason was no crime: Ludwig Beck, Chief of the German General Staff *(London: Kimber 1976), 317p.*

ROUBICZEK, Paul
Across the abyss: diary entries for the year, 1939—1940 *(Cambridge: CUP 1982), 325p.*

SCHEURIG, Bode
Free Germany *(Middletown, Conn: Wesleyan UP 1970), 311p.*

SCHMELING, E M
Flee the wolf: the story of a family's miraculous journey to freedom *(Virginia Beach, Va: Donning 1978), 290p.*

SHARP, Tony
The wartime Alliance and the zonal division of Germany *(Oxford: Clarendon 1975), 220p., bib.*

SHELTON, Regina M
To lose a war: Memories of a German girl *(Carbondale, Ill: Southern Illinois UP 1982), 228p.*

SIGNAL years of retreat, 1943—44: Hitler's wartime picture magazine *(New York: Prentice-Hall 1979), unp.*

SNYDER, Louis L
Encyclopaedia of the Third Reich *(London: Hale 1976), 410p., bib.*

WHITING, Charles
Hitler's werewolves *(New York: Playboy 1980), 220p.*
The home front — Germany *(Alexandria, Va: Time-Life 1982), 208p.*

WULFF, Wilhelm T H
Zodiac and swastika: how astrology guided Hitler's
Germany *(New York: Coward-McCann 1973), 192p.*

GERMAN AIR FORCE (LUFTWAFFE)

ADERS, Gebhard
History of the German night fighter force, 1917—1945
(London: Jane's 1979), 284p., bib.

BARKER, Arthur J
Ju-87 Stuka *(London: Arms & Armour 1980), 64p.*

BROWN, Eric M
Wings of the Luftwaffe: flying German aircraft of the
Second World War *(New York: Doubleday 1978), 176p.*

COOPER, Matthew
The German Air Force, 1933—1945: an anatomy of
failure *(London: Macdonald & Jane's 1981), 406p., bib.*

THE DEFENCE of the Reich *(London: Arms & Armour
1982), 232p.*

DIERICH, Wolfgang
Kampfgeschwader Edelweiss: the history of a German
bomber unit, 1935—45 *(London: Ian Allan 1975), 128p.*

ETHELL, Jeffrey L
The German jets in combat *(London: Macdonald & Jane's
1979), 143p., bib.*
Komet: the Messerschmitt 163 *(London: Ian Allan 1978),
160p.*

FABER, Harold *ed.*
Luftwaffe: a history *(New York: Times 1977), 267p.*

GERMAN Maritime aircraft *(Cambridge: Stephens 1980),
96p.*

GIRBIG, Werner
Six months to oblivion: the eclipse of the Luftwaffe
fighter force *(New York: Hippocrene 1975), 140p.*

GREEN, William
Augsberg eagle: the story of the Messerschmitt 109 *(London: Macdonald 1971), 128p.*
Warplanes of the Third Reich *(London: Macdonald 1970), 672p.*

HELD, Werner
Fighter!: Luftwaffe fighter planes and pilots *(London: Arms & Armour 1979), 224p.*
US title: The defence of the Reich

IRVING, David
The rise and fall of the Luftwaffe: the life of Luftwaffe Marshal Erhard Milch *(London: Weidenfeld & Nicolson 1974), 472p., bib.*

ISHOVEN, Armand van
The Luftwaffe in the Battle of Britain *(London: Ian Allan 1980), 128p.*
Messerschmitt BF 109 at war *(London: Ian Allan 1977), 160p.*

THE LUFTWAFFE *(Alexandria, Va: Time-Life 1982), 176p.*

MACKSEY, K
Kesselring: the making of the Luftwaffe *(London: Batsford 1978), 262p.*

MASON, Francis K
German warplanes of World War II *(Feltham, Mx: Temple 1983), 80p.*

MASTERS, David
German jet genesis *(London: Jane's 1982), 142p.*

MERRICK, K A
German aircraft markings, 1939—1945 *(London: Ian Allan 1977), 192p.*

MUNSON, Kenneth
German aircraft of World War 2 in colour *(Poole, Dorset: Blandford 1978), 160p.*

MUSCIANO, Walter A
Messerschmitt aces *(New York: Arco 1982), 217p.*

NIELSEN, Andreas
The German Air Force General Staff *(New York: Arno 1968), 265p.*

PEGG, Martin
Luftwaffe ground attack units, 1939—45 *(London: Osprey 1977), 48p.*

POOLMAN, Kenneth
Scourge of the Atlantic: Focke-Wulf Condor *(London: Macdonald & Jane's 1978), 192p.*

PRICE, Alfred
Focke Wulf 190 at war *(London: Ian Allan 1977), 160p.*
Luftwaffe handbook, 1939—1945 *(London: Ian Allan 1977), 111p.*
German Air Force bombers of World War II *(Leatherhead, Sy: Lacy 1969), 64p.*

ROBERTSON, Bruce
JU-87 Stuka *(Cambridge: Stephens 1977), 96p.*

RUDEL, Hans U
Stuka pilot *(London: Bantam 1979), 290p.*

SCHLIEPHAKE, Manfried
The birth of the Luftwaffe *(London: Ian Allan 1971), 88p.*

SCUTTS, Jerry
Luftwaffe night fighter units, 1939—45 *(London: Osprey 1978), 48p.*

SHEPHERD, Christopher
German aircraft of World War II with colour photographs *(London: Sidgwick & Jackson 1975), 144p.*

SHORES, Christopher
Luftwaffe fighter units: Russia 1941—45 *(London: Osprey 1978), 48p.*

SMITH, John R *and* CREEK, E J
Jet planes of the Third Reich *(Boylston, Mass: Monogram Aviation 1982), 400p.*

SMITH, John R *and* KAY, A L
German aircraft of the Second World War *(New York: Putnam 1978), 746p.*

STAHL, P W
KG 200: the true story *(London: Jane's 1981), 206p.*

STEINHOFF, Johannes
The last chance: the pilots' last chance against Goering, 1944—1945 *(London: Hutchinson 1977), 204p.*

VANAGS-BAGINSKIS, Alex
Stuka JU-87 *(London: Jane's 1982), 55p.*

WAKEFIELD, Kenneth
The first pathfinder: the operational history of Kampf-gruppe 100, 1939—1941 *(London: Kimber 1981), 256p.*
Luftwaffe encore: a study of two attacks in September 1940 *(London: Kimber 1980), 223p., bib.*

WEST, K S
The captive Luftwaffe *(London: Putnam 1977), 146p.*

WINDROW, Francis K
German Air Force fighters of World War Two *(Windsor, Berks: Lacy 1968), 2 vols.*

WOOD, Tony *and* GUNSTON, Bill
Hitler's Luftwaffe: a pictorial history and technical encyclopaedia of Hitler's air power in World War II *(London: Salamander 1977), 248p.*

GERMAN ARMY

BRETT-SMITH, Richard
Hitler's Generals *(London: Osprey 1976), 306p., bib.*

CHAMBERLAIN, Peter *and others*
German fighting vehicles, 1939—1945 *(London: Phoebus 1975), 64p.*

COOPER, Matthew
The German Army, 1933—1945: its political and military failure *(London: Macdonald & Jane's 1978), 598p., bib.*

DOWNING, David
The devil's virtuoso: German Generals at war, 1940—45 *(London: New English Library 1977), 256p., bib.*

FARRAR-HOCKLEY, A H
Student *(New York: Ballantine 1973), 158p.*

GERMAN Order of battle 1944: the Regiments, Formations and Units of the German ground forces *(London: Arms & Armour 1975), 496p.*

HARTMAN, Theodor
Wehrmacht Divisional signs, 1938—1945 *(London: Almark 1970), 88p.*

HITLER'S Generals and their battles *(London: Salamander 1978), 248p.*

HUMBLE, Richard
Hitler's Generals *(London: Panther 1976), 173p.*

KONSALIK, Heinz G
The heart of the 6th Army *(Henley-on-Thames, Oxon: Ellis 1977), 298p.*

LUCAS, James
Alpine elite: German mountain troops of World War II *(London: Macdonald & Jane's 1980), 226p., bib.*

MACKSEY, Kenneth
Guderian: Panzer General *(London: Macdonald & Jane's 1975), 226p., bib.*
US title: Guderian: creator of the Blitzkrieg

MELLENTHIN, F W von
German Generals of World War II: as I saw them *(Norman, Okla: University of Oklahoma 1977), 300p.*

MESSENGER, C
The art of Blitzkrieg *(London: Ian Allan 1976), 256p., bib.*

MILSOM, John
German half-tracked vehicles of World War 2: unarmoured support vehicles of the German Army, 1933—45 *(London: Arms & Armour 1975), 96p.*

OLIVER, Tony L
German motorcycles of World War II *(London: Almark 1978), 52p.*

O'NEILL, Robert J
The German Army and the Nazi Party, 1933–1939 *(London: Cassell 1966), 286p.*

REYNOLDS, Nicholas
Treason was no crime: Ludwig Beck, Chief of the German General Staff *(London: Kimber 1976), 317p.*

SEATON, Albert
The German Army, 1933–1945 *(London:Weidenfeld & Nicolson 1982), 310p., bib.*

THORWALD, Jungen
The illusion: Soviet soldiers in Hitler's armies *(New York: Harcourt 1975), 342p.*

WHITING, Charles
Siegfried: the Nazi's last stand *(London: Secker & Warburg 1982), 288p.*

(Panzers)

BARKER, A J
Panzers at war *(London: Ian Allan 1977), 160p.*

BENDER, Roger J
'Hermann Goering' from Regiment to Fallschirm Panzer-korps *(London: History Bookshop 1975), 208p., bib.*

CHAMBERLAIN, Peter *and* DOYLE, Hilary
Encyclopaedia of German tanks of World War Two *(London: Arms & Armour 1978), 272p.*

COOPER, Matthew
Panzer: the armoured force of the Third Reich *(London: Macdonald & Jane's 1976), 160p., bib.*

ELLIS, Christopher *and* CHAMBERLAIN, Peter
German tanks and fighting vehicles of World War II *(London: Phoebus 1976), 127p.*

HASTINGS, Max
Das Reich: the march of the 2nd SS Panzer Division through France *(New York: Holt 1982), 264p.*

LUCAS, James S
Germany's elite Panzer force: Grossdeutschland *(London: Macdonald & Jane's 1978), 152p.*

MELLENTHIN, Friedrich W von
Panzer battles: a study of the employment of armor in the Second World War *(Norman, Okla: University of Oklahoma 1982), 383p.*

PANZER Divisions of World War 2 *(Windsor, Berks: Profile 1976), 64p.*

PANZERS In the Balkans and Italy *(Cambridge: Stephens 1981), 96p.*

REDMON, Ronald L *and* CUCCARESE, J F
Panzergrenadiers in action *(Carrolton, Tex: Squadron Signal 1980), 50p.*

SENGER UND ETTERLIN, F M von
German tanks of World War Two: a complete illustrated history of German armoured fighting vehicles, 1926—1945 *(London: Arms & Armour 1969), 214p.*

WHITE, B T
German tanks and armoured vehicles, 1914—1945 *(London: Ian Allan 1966), 78p.*

[*see also TANKS*]

(Waffen SS)

BARKER, A J
Waffen SS at war *(London: Ian Allan 1982), 128p.*

BUSS, Philip H *and* MOLLO, Andrew
Hitler's Germanic Legions: an illustrated history of the Western European Legions with the SS, 1941—1943 *(London: Macdonald & Jane's), 144p., bib.*

GRABER, G S
History of the SS *(London: Hale 1978), 241p.*

HOLZMANN-WALTHER, Karl
Manual of the Waffen SS: badges, uniforms, equipment *(Watford, Herts: Argus 1976), 96p.*

INFIELD, Glenn B
Secrets of the SS *(New York: Stein & Day 1982), 271p.*

LUCAS, James *and* COOPER, M
Hitler's elite: Leinstandarte SS, 1939—45 *(London: Macdonald & Jane's 1975), 160p., bib.*

MOLLO, Andrew *comp.*
A pictorial history of the SS, 1923—1945 *(London: Macdonald & Jane's 1976), 192p., bib.*

QUARRIE, Bruce *comp.*
Waffen SS in Russia: a selection of German wartime photos *(Cambridge: Stephens 1978), 95p.*

SYDNOR, Charles W *jun.*
Soldiers of destruction: the SS Death's Head Division, 1933—1945 *(Princeton, NJ: Princeton UP 1977), 371p.*

GERMAN NAVY

BROWN, David
Tirpitz the floating fortress *(London: Arms & Armour 1977), 160p.*

COOKSLEY, Peter G
Operation Thunderbolt: the Nazi warships escape, 1942 *(London: Hale 1981), 190p.*

GERMAN Destroyers and escorts *(Cambridge: Stephens 1981), 96p.*

KEMP, Peter K
The escape of the Scharnhorst and Gneisenau *(London: Ian Allan 1975), 96p.*

KENNEDY, Ludovic
Menace: the life and death of the Tirpitz *(London: Sidgwick & Jackson 1979), 176p., bib.*
US title: The death of the Tirpitz

LENTON, Henry T
German warships of the Second World War *(London: Macdonald & Jane's 1975), 397p., bib.*

MUGGENTHALER, August K
German raiders of World War II: the first complete history of German ocean marauders *(London: Hale 1978), 308p., bib.*

MULLENHEIM-RECHBERG, B
Battleship Bismarck *(Annapolis, Md: Naval Institute 1980), 334p.*

SCHMALENBACH, Paul
German raiders: a history of auxiliary cruisers of the German Navy, 1895–1945 *(Annapolis, Md: Naval Institute 1979), 144p.*

SHOWELL, Jack P M
The German Navy in World War Two *(London: Arms & Armour 1979), 224p.*

STERN, Robert C
Kriegsmarine: a pictorial history of the German Navy, 1935–1945 *(London: Arms & Armour 1979), 80p.*

TAYLOR, J C
German warships of World War II *(London: Ian Allan 1966), 168p.*

VON DER PORTEN, Edward P
The German Navy in World War II *(New York: Galahad 1975), 274p.*

WHITLEY, M J
German destroyers in World War Two *(London: Arms & Armour 1983), 300p.*

WINTON, John
The death of the Scharnhorst *(Chichester, Sx: Bird 1983), 236p.*

[*see also BATTLESHIPS, CRUISERS, E-BOATS, U-BOATS*]

GESTAPO

FRIEDLAENDER, Saul
Kurt Gerstein: the ambiguity of good *(New York: Knopf 1969), 228p.*
UK title: Counterfeit Nazi

HOHNE, Heinz
The Order of the Death's Head: the story of Hitler's SS *(New York: Coward-McCann 1970), 688p.*

KOGON, Eugene
Theory and practice of hell *(New York: Octogon 1980), 307p.*

[*see also WAR CRIMES, WAR TRIALS*]

GOEBBELS

GOEBBELS, Joseph
The Goebbels diaries, 1939—1941 *(New York: Putnam 1983), 490p.*
The Goebbels diaries: the last days *(London: Secker & Warburg 1978), 368p.*

REIMANN, Viktor
The man who created Hitler: Joseph Goebbels *(London: Kimber 1977), 352p.*

GREECE

AUTY, Phyllis *and* CLOGG, R
British policy towards wartime resistance in Yugoslavia and Greece *(London: Barnes & Noble 1975), 308p.*

COUVARAS, Costa G
Photo album of the Greek resistance *(San Francisco, Cal: Wire 1978), 138p.*

CRUICKSHANK, Charles
Greece, 1940—1941 *(London: Davis-Poynter 1976), 206p., bib.*

HAMMOND, Nicholas
Venture into Greece: with the guerrillas, 1943—1944 *(London: Kimber 1983), 207p.*

HOWELL, Edward
Escape to live *(London: Grosvenor 1981), 217p.*

MAULE, Henry
Scobie, hero of Greece: the British campaign, 1944—45 *(London: Barker 1975), 285p.*

PAPASTRATIS, Procopis
British policy during the Second World War, 1941—1944 *(Cambridge: CUP 1983), 262p.*

SARAFIS, Stefanos
ELAS: Greek mountain army *(London: Merlin 1980), 556p.*

TURNER, Don
Kircakos: a British partisan in wartime Greece *(London: Hale 1982), 191p.*

WOODHOUSE, C M
The struggle for Greece, 1941—1945 *(London: Hart-Davis-McGibbon 1976), 316p., bib.*

GUADALCANAL

HOYT, Edwin P
Guadalcanal *(New York: Stein & Day 1982), 322p.*

LEE, Robert E
Victory at Guadalcanal *(Novata, Cal: Presidio 1981), 269p.*

MERILLAT, Herbert C
The island: a history of the 1st Marine Division on Guadalcanal, Aug.7—Dec.9, 1942 *(New York: Zenger 1979), 283p.*
Guadalcanal remembered *(New York: Dodd 1982), 332p.*

TANAKA, R
Japan's losing struggle for Guadalcanal *(Annapolis, Md: Naval Institute 1956)*

[see also PACIFIC, SOLOMON ISLANDS, US MARINES]

HALSEY

MERRILL, James A
A sailor's admiral: a biography of William F. Halsey *(New York: Crowell 1976), 271p.*

HAMBURG

MIDDLEBROOK, Martin
The battle of Hamburg: Allied bomber forces against a German city in 1943 *(London: Lane 1980), 424p., bib.*

MUSGROVE, Gordon
Operation Gomorrah: the Hamburg firestorm raids *(London: Macdonald & Jane's 1981), 197p.*

HAWAII

BEEKMAN, Allan
The Niihau incident *(Honolulu, Hawaii: Heritage 1982), 126p.*

HESS

DOUGLAS-HAMILTON, James
Motive for a mission: the story behind Rudolf Hess's flight
to Britain *(London: Macmillan 1971), 329p., bib.*

HEYDRICH

DESCHAER, Gunthe
Heydrich *(London: Orbis 1981), 351p., bib.*

HIMMLER

MANVELL, Roger *and* FRAENKEL H
Heinrich Himmler *(London: Heinemann 1965), 284p.*

HIROSHIMA [see ATOM BOMB]

HISTORY (general)

BALDWIN, Hanson W
The crucial years, 1939–1941: the world at war *(London:
Weidenfeld & Nicolson 1976), 499p.*

BALL, Adrian
The last day of the old world *(Westport, Conn: Greenwood
1978), 278p.*

BAUER, Eddy
The history of World War II *(London: Orbis 1979), 680p.*

CARVER, *Sir* Michael *ed.*
The war lords: military commanders of the twentieth
century *(London: Weidenfeld & Nicolson 1976), 624p.*

CHANT, Christopher *and others*
World War II: land, sea and air battles, 1939–1945 *(London: St Michael 1977), 253p.*

COLLIER, Richard
Armageddon *(London: Hamilton 1981), 310p., bib.*
The war that Stalin won *(London: Hamilton 1983), 320p.*
The world in flames *(London: Hamilton 1979), 258p., bib.*
US title: 1940: the avalanche

COOK, Graeme
Survival against all odds *(London: Harwood-Smart 1975), 147p.*

DEIGHTON, Len
Blitzkrieg, from the rise of Hitler to the fall of Dunkirk *(London: Cape 1979), 320p.*

DOUGLAS, Roy
The advent of war, 1939 *(London: Macmillan 1978), 67p., bib.*
New alliances, 1940–41 *(London: Macmillan 1982), 154p., bib.*

EGGLESTON, G T
Roosevelt, Churchill and the World War II opposition *(Old Greenwich, Conn: Devlin-Adair 1979), 255p.*

GOODSPEED, D J
The German wars, 1914–1945 *(London: Orbis 1978), 561p.*

HEIFERMAN, Ronald
World War II *(New York: Octopus 1975), 256p.*

HERRIDGE, Charles
Pictorial history of World War II *(London: Hamlyn 1975), 253p.*

THE HISTORY of the Second World War *(London: Phoebus 1978), 464p.*

JABLONSKI, Edward
A pictorial history of the World War II years *(New York: Doubleday 1977), 319p.*

LAQUEUR, Walter
The Second World War: essays in military and political history *(London: Sage 1982), 407p.*

LONGMATE, Norman
When we won the war: the story of victory in Europe, 1945 *(London: Hutchinson 1977), 194p.*

LUKACS, John A
The last European war: Sept. 1939—Dec. 1941 *(London: Routledge & Kegan Paul 1976), 562p., bib.*

LYALL, Gavin *and* LYALL, Bernard
Operation warboard, wargaming World War II battles in 20—25 mm scale *(New York: McKay 1977), 159p.*

MICHEL, Henri
The Second World War *(London: Deutsch 1975), 947p., bib.*

RIGGE, Simon
War in the outposts *(Alexandria, Va: Time-Life 1980), 208p.*

SCHACHTMAN, Tom
The phony war, 1939—1940 *(New York: Harper 1982), 289p.*

STANHOPE-PALMER, Roger
World War II: some decisive episodes *(Ilfracombe, Devon: Stockwell 1979), 151p., bib.*

STOKESBURY, James L
A short history of World War II *(New York: Morrow 1980), 420p., bib.*

TAYLOR, Alan J P
The Second World War: an illustrated history *(New York: Putnam 1975), 234p.*

WEINBERG, Gerhard
World in the balance: behind the scenes of World War II *(Hanover, NH: University of New England 1981), 165p., bib.*

YOUNG, Peter
World War II *(London: Hamlyn 1980), 249p.*
[*see also PHOTOGRAPHY*]

HITLER

CECIL, Robert
Hitler's decision to invade Russia, 1941 *(London: Davis-Poynter 1975), 192p.*

DEUTSCH, Harold C
Hitler and his Generals: the hidden crisis, January—June 1938 *(Minneapolis: University of Minneapolis 1974), 452p., bib.*

FEST, Joachim C
Hitler *(New York: Harcourt 1974), 844p.*

GILBERT, Felix *ed.*
Hitler directs his war: the secret records of his daily military conferences *(Toronto: OUP 1950), 187p.*

HESTON, Leonard L *and* HESTON, Renate
The medical casebook of Adolf Hitler *(London: Kimber 1979), 184p., bib.*

INFIELD, Glenn B
Hitler's secret life *(London: Hamlyn 1980), 285p.*
Eva and Adolf *(New York: Grosset 1974), 330p., bib.*

IRVING, David *ed.*
Adolf Hitler: the medical diaries *(London: Sidgwick & Jackson 1983), 310p.*
Hitler's war *(London: Hodder & Stoughton 1977), 926p., bib.*

MASON, Herbert M
To kill Hitler *(London: Joseph 1979), 313p., bib.*

RICH, Norman
Hitler's war aims: ideology *(New York: Norton 1976), vol.I.*

STEEH, Judith
The rise and fall of Adolf Hitler *(London: Hamlyn & Bison 1980), 192p.*

STEINERT, M G
Hitler's war and the Germans: public mood and attitude during the 2nd World War *(Athens, Ohio: Ohio University 1977), 387p.*

STERN, Joseph P
Hitler: the Fuhrer and the people *(London: Fontana 1975), 254p.*

STONE, Norman
Hitler *(London: Hodder & Stoughton 1980), 195p.*

TOLAND, John
Adolf Hitler *(New York: Doubleday 1976), 1035p.*
Hitler: the pictorial documentary of his life *(London: Hutchinson 1979), 204p.*

WALTHER, Herbert *ed.*
Der Fuhrer: the life and times of Adolf Hitler *(London: Bison 1978), 255p.*

HOLLAND

ROELFZEMA, Erik H
Soldier of orange *(London: Sphere 1981), 224p.*

ROSE, Leesha
The tulips are red *(London: Yoseloff 1979), 275p.*

VOUTE, Peter
Only a free man: war memories of two Dutch doctors, 1940–1945 *(Santa Fey, NM: Lightning Tree 1982), 188p.*

HOME GUARD

GULVIN, K R
Kent Home Guard: a history *(Rochester, Kent: North Kent Books 1980), 92p., bib.*

HONG KONG

ENDACOTT, G B *and* BIRCH, A *eds*
Hong Kong eclipse *(Oxford: OUP 1978), 428p.*

LINDSAY, Oliver
At the going down of the sun: Hong Kong and South East Asia 1941–45 *(London: Hamilton 1981), 258p., bib.*

The lasting honour: the fall of Hong Kong, 1941 *(London: Hamilton 1978), 226p., bib.*

RIDE, Edwin
BAAG: Hong Kong resistance 1942–1945 *(London: OUP 1982), 364p.*

HUNGARY

BIERMAN, John
Righteous gentile: the story of Raoul Wallenberg missing hero of the holocaust *(London: Lane 1981), 218p., bib.*

GRANT, Myrna
The journey *(London: Hodder & Stoughton 1979), 205p.*

LAMBERT, Gilles
Operation Hazalah *(Minneapolis: Bobbs-Merrill 1974), 235p.*

LESTER, Elenore
Wallenberg: the man in the iron web *(New York: Prentice-Hall 1982), 183p.*

MARTON, Kati
Wallenberg *(New York: Random House 1982), 243p.*

RELIEF In Hungary and the failure of the Joel Brand mission *(New York: Garland 1982), 249p.*

SIEGAL, Aranka
Upon the head of the goat: a childhood in Hungary, 1939–1944 *(New York: Farrar 1981), 213p.*

SZINAI, Miklos *and* SZUCS, Laszlo *eds.*
The confidential papers of Admiral Horthy *(Budapest: Corvina: 1965), 439p.*

WERBELL, Frederick E *and* CLARKE, T
Lost hero: the mystery of Raoul Wallenberg *(New York: McGraw-Hill 1982), 284p.*

INDIA

GORDINE, Ernest T C
A patriot's boast *(Ilfracombe, Devon: Stockwell 1975), 210p.*

INDIAN ARMY

LEVER, J C G
The sowas and the jawan: the soldiers of the former Indian Army and their homelands *(Ilfracombe, Devon: Stockwell 1981), 160p.*

PRASAD, Nandan *ed.*
The Indian Armed Forces in the Second World War: the North African campaign *(London: Longman 1956)*

INDONESIA

FALK, Stanley L
Seventy days to Singapore *(New York: Putnam 1975), 301p.*

JACOBS, Gideon F
Prelude to the monsoon: assignment in Sumatra *(Philadelphia, Pa: University of Pennsylvania 1982), 249p.*

INTELLIGENCE

BEESLY, Patrick
Very special intelligence: the story of the Admiralty's operational intelligence centre, 1939—1945 *(London: Hamilton 1977), 271p.*

CLAYTON, Aileen
The enemy is listening: the story of the Y service
(London: Hutchinson 1980), 381p., bib.

COLBY, William *and* FORBATH, Peter
Honourable men: my life in the CIA *(London: Hutchinson 1978), 493p.*

COLLIER, Basil
Hidden weapons *(London: Hamilton 1982), 320p.*

DE CHAMPLAIN, Helene
The secret war of Helene de Champlain *(London: W.H. Allen 1980), 275p.*

DULLES, Allen
The craft of intelligence *(New York: Harper 1963), 272p., bib.*

FRASER-SMITH, Charles
The secret war of Charles Fraser-Smith *(London: Joseph 1981), 159p.*

GLEESON, James
They feared no evil: the woman agents of Britain's secret armies, 1939—45 *(London: Hale 1976), 173p., bib.*

HAGEN, Louis E
The secret war for Europe: a dossier of espionage *(New York: Stein & Day 1969), 287p.*

HAMPSHIRE, A Cecil
Undercover sailors: secret operations of World War II *(London: Kimber 1981), 208p., bib.*

HINSLEY, F H *and others*
British Intelligence in the Second World War *(London: HMSO 1979—81), 2 vols.*

HYDE, H M
Secret intelligence agent *(London: Constable 1982), 281p.*

KIRKPATRICK, Lyman
The real CIA *(London: Macmillan 1968), 312p.*

LAWSON, Donald E
The secret World War II *(New York: Watts-Franklin 1978)*, *118p.*

LEASOR, James
Code name Nimrod *(Boston, Mass: Houghton-Mifflin 1981), 263p.*
UK title: The unknown warrior

MOSLEY, Leonard
The Druid *(London: Eyre Methuen 1982), 256p.*

PAINE, Lauran
The invisible world of espionage *(London: Hale 1976), 173p., bib.*

PESKETT, S John
Strange intelligence: from Dunkirk to Nuremberg *(London: Hale 1981), 208p.*

POWYS-LYBBC, Ursula
The eye of intelligence *(London: Kimber 1983), 223p.*

STANLEY, Roy M
World War II photo intelligence *(London: Sidgwick & Jackson 1982), 374p., bib.*

TREPPER, Leopold
The great game: the story of the Red Orchestra *(New York: McGraw-Hill 1976), 442p.*

VACHA, Robert
A spy for Churchill *(London: Everest 1974), 191p.*

VAN DER RHOER, Edward
Deadly magic: a personal account of communication intelligence in World War II in the Pacific *(New York: Scribner 1978), 225p.*

WEST, Nigel
MI6, British secret intelligence operations, 1904—45 *(London: Weidenfeld & Nicolson 1983), 266p.*

WHEATLEY, Dennis
The deception planners: my secret war *(London: Hutchinson 1980), 240p.*

WHITING, Charles
The battle for Twelveland: an account of Anglo-American intelligence operations within Nazi Germany, 1939—1945 *(London: Cooper 1975), 240p.*
US *title:* The spymasters

[*see also MAGIC, OSS, PURPLE, SECRET SERVICE, SOE, ULTRA*]

INTERNEES

CROUTER, Natalie
Forbidden diary: a record of wartime internment, 1941—1945 *(New York: Franklin 1980), 546p.*

GILLMAN, Peter *and* GILLMAN, Leni
"Collar the lot": how Britain interned and expelled its wartime refugees *(London: Quartet 1980), 334p., bib.*

LAFITTE, F
The internment of aliens *(London: Penguin 1940), 256p.*

STENT, Ronald
A bespattered page: the internment of His Majesty's most loyal enemy aliens *(London: Deutsch 1980), 282p., bib.*

UCHIDA, Yoshiko
Desert exile: the uprooting of a Japanese—American family *(Washington: University of Washington 1982), 154p.*

IRAQ

PAIFORCE: the official story of the Persia and Iraq Command, 1941—1946 *(London: HMSO 1948), 137p.*

WARNER, Geoffrey
Iraq and Syria, 1941 *(Newark, Del: University of Delaware 1980), 180p.*

IRELAND

CARROLL, Joseph T
Ireland in the war years *(Newton Abbot, Devon: David & Charles 1975), 190p.*

CARTER, Carolle J
The shamrock and the swastika: German espionage in Ireland in World War 2 *(Palo Alto, Cal: Pacific 1977), 287p.*

FISK, Robert
In time of war: a divided Ireland and Ulster in the Second World War *(London: Deutsch 1983), 500p.*

PRITTIE, T F
Through Irish eyes *(London: Bachman & Turner 1977), 320p.*

ITALY

ADAMS, H H
Italy at war *(Alexandria, Va: Time-Life 1982), 207p.*

HILL, Robert M *and* CRAIG, E
In the wake of war: memoirs of an Alabama military government officer in World War II, Italy *(Birmingham, Ala: University of Alabama 1982), 150p.*

KNOX, MacGregor
Mussolini unleashed, 1939—1941: politics and strategy in Fascist Italy's last war *(Cambridge: CUP 1982), 385p., bib.*

LEWIS, Norman
Naples 1944 *(London: Collins 1978), 206p.*

RAMATI, Alexander
While the Pope kept silent: Assisi and the Nazi occupation *(London: Allen & Unwin 1978), 181p.*
US title: The Assisi underground

REID, Ian
A game called survival: the story of Betty di San Marzano and her children in wartime Italy *(London: Evans 1980), 144p.*

SMITH, Eric D
Even the brave falter *(London: Hale 1978), 144p.*

TURRA, Mario
Mario *(Acworth, Ga: Names of Distinction 1975), 174p.*

WHITING, Douglas
Prisoners, people, places, partisans and patriots *(Bognor Regis, Sx: New Horizon 1980), 227p.*

ITALIAN AIR FORCE

GENTILLI, Roberto *and* GORENA, L
Macchi C.202 in action *(Carrelton, Tex: Squadron Signal 1980), 50p.*

ITALIAN CAMPAIGN

BLAXLAND, Gregory
Alexander's Generals: the Italian campaign, 1944—45 *(London: Kimber 1979), 320p.*

COLE, *Sir* David
Rough road to Rome: a foot-soldier in Sicily and Italy, 1943—44 *(London: Kimber 1983), 239p.*

GARLAND, A *and* SMYTH, H
Sicily and the surrender of Italy *(Washington DC: Dept of Army 1965)*

HARPUR, Brian
The impossible victory: a personal account of the battle for the River Po *(London: Kimber 1980), 202p.*

HARVEY, J M L
D-Day dodger *(London: Kimber 1979), 189p.*

HORSFALL, John
Fling our banner to the wind *(Kineton, War: Roundwood 1978), 225p.*

WALLACE, Robert
The Italian campaign *(Alexandria, Va: Time-Life 1978), 208p.*

[*see also BRITISH ARMY (EIGHTH ARMY), CASSINO, ROME, SALERNO, US ARMY*]

JAPAN

ARGYLE, Christopher J
Japan at war, 1937—45 *(London: Barker 1976), 224p.*

BARKER, Ralph
Against the sea *(London: Chatto & Windus 1972), 199p.*

COLLIER, Basil
Japan at war: an illustrated history of the war in the Far East, 1931—1945 *(London: Sidgwick & Jackson 1975), 192p.*

COOX, Alvin D
Tojo *(New York: Ballantine 1975), 160p., bib.*

CRIES For peace: experiences of Japanese victims of World War II *(Tokyo: Japan Times 1978), 234p.*

THE FATEFUL Choice: Japan's advance into South East Asia, 1939—41 *(New York: Columbia University 1980), 366p.*

GUILLAIN, Robert
I saw Tokyo burning *(London: Murray 1981), 320p.*

HARRINGTON, Joseph D
Yankee Sumarai: the secret role of Nisei in America's Pacific victory *(Detroit, Mich: Pettigrew 1979), 383p.*

HAVENS, Thomas R
Valley of darkness: the Japanese people and World War II *(New York: Norton 1978), 280p.*

JAPAN's Greater East Asia co-prosperity sphere in World War II: selected readings and documents *(London: OUP 1975), 212p., bib.*

MAYER, S L *ed.*
The Japanese war machine *(London: Hamlyn 1976), 255p.*

PICCIGAILO, Philip R
The Japanese on trial: Allied war crimes operations in the East, 1945−1951 *(Austin, Tex: University of Texas 1979), 292p.*

SHIROYAMA, Saburo
War criminal: the life and death of Hirota Koki *(Tokyo: Kodansha 1977), 301p.*

WEBBER, Bert
Retaliation: Japanese attacks and Allied countermeasures on the Pacific coast in World War II *(Corvallis, Ore: Oregon State University 1975), 178p.*

WHEELER, Keith
Bombers over Japan *(Alexandria, Va: Time-Life 1982), 208p.*
The fall of Japan *(Alexandria, Va: Time-Life 1983), 207p.*

ZICH, Arthur
The rising sun *(Alexandria, Va: Time-Life 1977), 208p.*

JAPANESE AIR FORCE

COLLIER, Basil
Japanese aircraft of World War II *(London: Sidgwick & Jackson 1979), 144p.*

FRANCILLON, Rene J
Japanese aircraft of the Pacific war *(New York: Putnam 1979), 570p.*

INOGUCHI, Rikihei *and* PINEAU, R
The divine wind: Japan's kamikaze force in World War II *(Westport, Conn: Greenwood 1978), 224p.*

MIKESH, Robert C
Zero fighter *(London: Macdonald & Jane's 1981), 56p.*

OKUMIYA, M *and others*
Zero!: the air war in the Pacific during World War II, from the Japanese viewpoint *(Washington DC: Zenger 1979), 424p.*

O'NEILL, Richard
Suicide squads, World War II *(New York: St Martin's 1982), 246p.*

WILLMOTT, Hedley P
Mitsubishi A6M Zero *(London: Arms & Armour 1980), 64p.*

WORLD WAR II: US Navy and Japanese combat planes *(Blue Ridge, Pa: TAB 1981)*

JAPANESE ARMY

BARKER, A J
Japanese Army handbook, 1939—1945 *(London: Ian Allan 1979), 128p.*

MARKHAM, George
Japanese infantry weapons of World War II *(London: Arms & Armour 1976), 96p.*

JAPANESE NAVY

AGAWA, Hiroyuki
The reluctant admiral: Yamamoto and the Imperial Navy *(Tokyo: Kodansha 1979), 397p.*

BARKER, A J
Yamashita *(New York: Ballantine 1973), 159p.*

DULL, Paul S
A battle history of the Imperial Japanese Navy, 1941—1945 *(Annapolis, Md: Naval Institute 1978), 402p.*

FRANCILLON, Rene J
Imperial Japanese Navy bombers of World War II
(Leatherhead, Sy: Lacy 1969), 64p.

HOWARTH, Stephen
Morning glory: the drama of the Imperial Japanese Navy
(London: Hamilton 1983), 384p.

ORITA, Zenji *and* HARRINGTON, J D
I-boat captain *(Canoga Park, Cal: Major 1976), 336p.*

SPURR, Russell
A glorious day to die: the kamikaze mission of the battleship Yamoto, April 1945 *(New York: Newmarket 1981),
341p.*

THOMAS, David A
Japan's war at sea: Pearl Harbor to the Coral Sea *(London:
Deutsch 1978), 222p., bib.*

WATTS, Anthony J *and* GORDON, Brian
The Imperial Japanese Navy *(London: Macdonald 1971),
529p.*

JAPANESE PRISON CAMPS

COLEMAN, John S
Bataan and beyond: memories of an American P.O.W.
(College Station, Tex: Texas A & M 1978), 210p.

FISHER, Charles A
Three times a guest: recollections of Japan and the
Japanese *(London: Cassell 1980), 272p.*

GORDON, Harry
Die like the carp *(Stanmore, NSW Aust: Cassell 1978),
284p.*

GRASHIO, Samuel C *and* NORLING, B
Return to freedom: the war memoirs of . . . *(Tulsa, Okla:
MCN 1982), 166p.*

HALL, David O W
Prisoners of Japan *(Wellington, NZ: Dept of International Affairs 1949)*

HARRISON, Kenneth
Road to Hiroshima *(Adelaide, Aust: Rigby 1983), 280p. Previously published as:* The brave Japanese

LUCAS, Celia
Prisoners of Santo Tomas *(London: Cooper 1975), 220p.*

MacCARTHY, Aidan
A doctor's war *(London: Robson 1979), 159p.*

MACHI, Mario
The Emperor's hostages *(New York: Vantage 1982), 90p.*

MURPHY, John H
Call me tomorrow *(New York: Vantage 1978), 318p.*

PATKIN, Benzion
The Dunera internees *(London: Cassell 1979), 185p.*

POUNDER, Thomas
Death camps of the River Kwai *(St Ives, Cornwall: United Writers 1977), 262p.*

QUINN, Michael A
Love letters to Mike: 40 months as a Japanese prisoner of war, Apr. 9, 1942 to Sept. 17, 1945 *(New York: Vantage 1977), 331p.*

TOMPKINS, Lilian G
Three wasted years: women in Changi prison *(Hamilton, NZ: Tompkins 1977), 97p.*

WARNER, Lavinia *and* SANDILANDS, John
Women behind the wire: a story of prisoners of the Japanese, 1942–45 *(London: Joseph 1982), 289p., bib.*

WHITECROSS, Roy H
Slaves of the Sun of Heaven: the personal story of an Australian prisoner of the Japanese during the years 1941–1945 *(Sydney, Aust: Dymock n.d.), 255p.*

JAVA

JACKSON, Daphne
Java nightmare *(Padstow, Cornwall: Tabb House 1979)*, *156p.*

VAN OOSTEN, F C
The battle of the Java Sea *(London: Ian Allan 1976)*, *128p., bib.*

JEWS

AINSZTEIN, Reuben
Jewish resistance in Nazi-occupied Eastern Europe *(New York: Harper 1974)*, *970p.*

ALIAV, Ruth *and* MANN, Peggy
The last escape *(New York: Doubleday 1973)*, *559p.*

AURIEL, Ehud
Open the gates!: a personal story of illegal immigration to Israel *(London: Weidenfeld & Nicolson 1975)*, *370p.*

BAUER, Yehuda
American Jewry and the holocaust *(Detroit, Mich: Wayne State University 1981)*, *522p.*
From diplomacy to resistance: a history of Jewish Palestine 1939–1945 *(Philadelphia, Pa: Jewish 1970)*, *635p.*
The holocaust in historical perspective *(Seattle, Wash: University of Washington 1978)*, *181p.*
The Jewish emergence from powerlessness *(Toronto: Toronto University 1979)*, *89p.*

BAYFIELD, Tony
Churban: the murder of the Jews of Europe *(London: Michael Goulston 1981)*, *192p.*

BISS, Andreas
A million Jews to save: check to the final solution *(Cranbury, NJ: Barnes 1975)*, *271p.*

BLOOMBERG, Marty
The Jewish holocaust: an annotated guide to books in English *(New York: Borgo 1982), 192p.*

BRAND, Sandra
I dared to live *(New York: Shengold 1978), 204p.*

BUTLER, Rupert
Legions of death *(Feltham, Mx: Hamlyn 1983), 255p., bib.*

BUTZ, A R
The hoax of the twentieth century *(Richmond, Sy: Historical Review 1976), 315p., bib.*

CHOLAWSKI, Shalom
Soldiers from the ghetto *(New York: Tantivy 1980), 182p.*

DAWIDOWICZ, Lucy S
The war against the Jews, 1933–1945 *(London: Weidenfeld & Nicolson 1975), 550p., bib.*

DOBKOWSKI, Michael N *ed.*
The politics of indifference: a documentary history of holocaust victims in America *(Washington DC: University Press of America 1982), 473p.*

ECKMAN, Lester S *and* LAZAR, H
The Jewish resistance: the history of the Jewish partisans in Lithuania and White Russia during the Nazi-occupation, 1940–1945 *(New York: Shengold 1977), 282p.*

EHRENBURG, Ilya and GROSSMAN, V *eds.*
The Black Book: the ruthless murder of Jews by German–Fascist invaders, and in the death camps of Poland during the war of 1941–1945 *(New York: Schoken 1982), 596p.*

ELGEY, Georgette
The open window *(London: Woburn 1974), 212p.*

EZRAHI, Sidra D
By words alone: the holocaust *(Chicago: University of Chicago 1980), 262p.*

FEIN, Helen
Accounting for genocide: national responses and Jewish victimisation during the holocaust *(New York: Free Press 1979), 468p., bib.*

FERENCZ, Benjamin
Less than slaves: Jewish forced labor and the quest for compensation *(Cambridge, Mass: Harvard UP 1979), 249p.*

GILBERT, Martin
Atlas of the holocaust *(London: Joseph 1982), 256p., bib.*
Final journey: the fate of the Jews in Nazi Europe *(London: Allen & Unwin 1979), 224p.*

GRAY, Martin *and* GALLO, M
For those I loved *(London: Pan 1975), 349p.*

GROSS, Leonard
The last Jews in Berlin *(New York: Simon & Schuster 1982), 349p.*

GRUBER, Samuel
I chose life *(New York: Shengold 1978)*

GUTMAN, Yisrael
The Jews of Warsaw, 1939—1943 *(Brighton, Sx: Harvester 1982), 512p.*

HALLIE, Philip P
Lest innocent blood be shed: the story of the village of Le Chambon and how goodness happened there *(New York: Harper 1979), 304p.*

HELLMAN, Peter
Avenue of the righteous *(London: Dent 1981), 267p.*

KENEALLY, Thomas
Schindler's ark *(London: Hodder & Stoughton 1982), 576p.*

KRANZLER, David H
Japanese, Nazis and Jews: the Jewish refugee community of Shanghai, 1938—1945 *(New York: Sifria 1976), 644p.*

KUPER, Jack
Child of the holocaust *(New York: New American Library 1980), unp.*

KWINTA, Chara
I'm still living *(Toronto: Simon-Pierre 1974), 279p.*

LAQUEUR, Walter
The terrible secret: an investigation into the suppression of information about Hitler's final solution *(London: Weidenfeld & Nicolson 1980), 262p.*

LATOUR, Anny
The Jewish resistance in France, 1940—1944 *(New York: Holocaust Library 1981), 287p.*

MICHELSON, Frida
I survived Rumbuli *(New York: Holocaust Library 1982), 232p.*

POLIAKOV, Leon
Harvest of hate: the Nazi program for the destruction of the Jews of Europe *(New York: Holocaust Library 1979), 350p.*

REINGOLD, Henry L
The politics of rescue: the Roosevelt administration and the holocaust 1938—1945 *(New York: Holocaust Library 1970), 432p.*

RELIEF And rescue of Jews from Nazi oppression, 1943—1945 *(New York: Garland 1982), 242p.*

RESCUE To Switzerland: the Mussy and Saly Mayer affair *(New York: Garland 1982), 219p.*

ROITER, Howard
Voices from the holocaust *(New York: William-Frederick 1975), 221p.*

ROSE, Leesha
The tulips are red *(Cranbury, NJ: Barnes 1978), 275p.*

ROSENFELD, Alvin H
A double dying: reflections and holocaust *(Bloomington, Ind: Indiana University 1980), 216p.*

SCHWIEFERT, Peter
The bird has no wings: letters *(New York: St Martin's 1975), 180p.*

SEIDEL, Gill
The holocaust denial *(London: Pluto 1983), 128p.*

STEINBERG, Lucien
Not as a lamb: the Jews against Hitler *(Farnborough, Hants: Saxon 1974), 358p.*

SVIRSKY, Grigory
Hostages: the personal testimony of a Soviet Jew *(New York: Knopf 1976), 305p.*

SYRKIN, Marie
Blessed is the match: the story of Jewish resistance *(Philadelphia, Pa: Jewish Publication Society of America 1977), 366p.*

SZAJKOWSKI, Zosa
Jews and the French Foreign Legion *(New York: Ktav 1975), 280p.*

SZCHORY, E
Night is day: memoirs of a prisoner of war and a partisan *(New York: Vantage 1979), 84p.*

TEMCHIN, Michael
The witch doctor: memoirs of a partisan *(New York: Holocaust Library 1983), 184p.*

TOKAYER, Marvin *and* SWARTZ, Mary
The Jugu plan: the untold story of the Japanese and the Jews during World War II *(London: Paddington 1979), 287p.*

TREPMAN, Paul
Among men and beasts *(London: Yoseloff 1979), 229p.*

TRUNK, Isaiah
Jewish responses to Nazi persecution: collective and individual behaviour in extremis *(New York: Stein & Day 1979), 371p.*
Judenrat: the Jewish Councils in Eastern Europe under Nazi occupation *(New York: Stein & Day 1977)*

VISHNIAC, Roman
A vanished world *(London: Ian Allan 1983), vol.I*

WASSERSTEIN, Bernard
Britain and the Jews of Europe, 1939—1945 *(Oxford: Clarendon 1979), 389p., bib.*

WIESENTHAL, Simon
The sun flower: with a symposium *(New York: Schocken 1977), 216p.*
Max and Helen *(London: Granada 1982), 122p.*

[see also CONCENTRATION CAMPS, HUNGARY, POLAND, RESISTANCE]

KAMIKAZE

INOGUCHI, Rikihei *and* PINEAU, R
The divine wind: Japan's Kamikaze Force in World War II *(Westport, Conn: Greenwood 1978), 224p.*

O'NEILL, Richard
Suicide squads, World War II *(New York: St Martin's 1982), 296p.*

WARNER, Denis A *and others*
The sacred warriors: Japan's suicide legions *(New York: Nostrand 1982), 370p.*

[see also JAPANESE AIR FORCE]

KATYN WOOD

FITZGIBBON, Louis
Unpitied and unknown: Katyn-Bologoye-Dergachi *(London: Bachman & Turner 1975), 496p.*

MLYNASKI, Bronislaw
The 79th survivor *(London: Bachman & Turner 1976), 246p.*

KENT

ROOTES, Andrew
Front line county *(London: Hale 1980), 223p., bib.*

KING (Admiral)

BUELL, Thomas B
Master of sea power: a biography of Fleet Admiral Ernest J. King *(Boston, Mich: Little, Brown 1980), 609p.*

LANDING CRAFT
[see AMPHIBIOUS WARFARE, NORMANDY]

LEYTE

DAVIDSON, Orlando R
The deadeyes: the story of the 96th Infantry Division *(Nashville, Tenn: Battery 1981), 310p.*

HOYT, Edwin P
The battle of Leyte Gulf: the death knell of the Japanese Fleet *(New York: Playboy 1979), 346p.*

STEWART, Adrian
Battle of Leyte Gulf *(London: Hale 1979), 223p., bib.*

[see also PACIFIC, UNITED STATES NAVY]

LITERATURE

HARRIS, Frederick J
Encounters with darkness: French and German writers on World War II *(Oxford: OUP 1983), 384p.*

LONDON

BELL, R W
The bull's eye *(London: Cassell 1943), 94p.*

BLAKE, Lewis
Bromley in the front line: the story of the London Borough of Bromley under enemy attack in the Second World War *(Whitstable, Kent: Blake 1980), 88p.*
Red alert: South East London: the former Metropolitan Boroughs of Deptford, Greenwich, Lewisham and Woolwich under air attack during the long years of the Second World War *(Bromley, Kent: Blake 1982), 106p.*

GRANT, Ian *and* MADDREN, Nicholas
The city at war *(London: Joseph 1975), 128p.*

HEWISON, Robert
Under siege: literary life in London, 1939—45 *(London: Weidenfeld & Nicolson 1977), 219p.*

JOHNSON, David
The city ablaze: the second great fire of London, 29th December 1940 *(London: Kimber 1980), 217p.*

NIXON, Barbara
Raiders overhead *(Banbury, Oxon: Gulliver 1980), 176p.*

LONG RANGE DESERT GROUP

JENNER, Bob
Long Range Desert Group *(London: Osprey 1983), 40p.*

OWEN, David L
Providence their guide: the Long Range Desert Group, 1940—45 *(London: Harrap 1980), 256p.*

MACARTHUR

HUNT, Frazier
The untold story of Douglas MacArthur *(London: Hale 1954), 533p.*

JAMES, D C
The years of MacArthur *(London: Cooper 1970), 2 vols.*

MANCHESTER, William
American Caesar: Douglas MacArthur *(London: Hutchinson 1979), 793p.*

MAGIC

COCHRAN, Alexander S
The MAGIC diplomatic summaries *(New York: Garland 1982), 139p.*

LEWIN, Ronald
The American MAGIC *(London: Penguin 1983), 332p.*

MALAYSIA

KELLY, T
Hurricane over the jungle *(London: Kimber 1977), 234p.*

TRENOWDEN, Ian
Operations most secret: SOE the Malayan theatre *(London: Kimber 1978), 231p.*

MALTA

ATTARD, Joseph
The battle of Malta *(London: Kimber 1980), 252p., bib.*

DOUGLAS-HAMILTON, James
The air battle for Malta: the diaries of a fighter pilot *(Edinburgh: Mainstream 1981), 208p., bib.*

HOGAN, George
Malta: the triumphant years, 1940—1942 *(London: Hale 1978), 208p.*

JACKSON, Robert
Malta victory: yeoman on the George Cross Island *(London: Barker 1980), 173p.*

POOLMAN, Kenneth
Night strike from Malta: 830 Squadron Royal Navy and Rommel's convoys *(London: Jane's 1980), 192p., bib.*

MANPOWER

FLYNN, George Q
The mess in Washington; manpower, mobilization in World War II *(Westport, Conn: Greenwood 1979), 294p.*

MARSHALL

MOSLEY, Leonard
Marshall: organizer of victory *(London: Methuen 1982), 608p.*

MEDICAL

AMOSOV, Nikolai M
PPG-2266: a surgeon's war *(New York: Regnery 1975), 261p.*

BATY, John A
Surgeon in the jungle war *(London: Kimber 1979), 196p.*

BRIGGS, I G
They gave me a crown: the diversions of a doctor in war and peace *(London: Jenkins 1944), 220p.*

KUNZ, Egon C
The intruders: refugee doctors in Australia *(Canberra, Aust: Australian National UP 1975), 139p.*

MacCARTHY, Aidan
A doctor's war *(London: Robson 1979), 159p.*

MEDITERRANEAN

FEATHERSTONE, Donald F
A wargamer's guide to the Mediterranean campaigns, 1943—1945 *(Cambridge: Stephens 1977), 152p.*

GILLMAN, Ronald E
The shiphunters *(London: Murray 1976), 241p.*

WHIPPLE, Addison B C
The Mediterranean *(Alexandria, Va: Time-Life 1981), 208p.*

MEMOIRS

AMERY, Julian
Approach march: a venture in autobiography *(London: Hutchinson 1973), 456p.*

BOHLEN, Charles E
Witness to history, 1929—1969 *(New York: Norton 1973), 562p.*

(DONITZ, Karl) PADFIELD, Peter
Donitz *(London: Gollancz 1983), 560p.*

GEYR von SCHWEPPENBURG, Leo
The critical years *(London: Wingate 1952), 207p.*

(HANKEY, Maurice *1st baron*) ROSKILL, S
Hankey, man of secrets *(London: Collins 1974), vol.3.*

(HOBART, *Sir* Percy) MACKSEY, Kenneth
Armoured crusader: Major-General Sir Percy Hobart *(London: Hutchinson 1967), 348p.*

(ISMAY, Hastings L *1st baron*) WINGATE, *Sir* Ronald
Lord Ismay *(London: Hutchinson 1970), 232p.*

MASTERMAN, *Sir* John C
On the chariot wheel *(London: OUP 1975), 384p.*

MUGGERIDGE, Malcolm
Chronicles of wasted time *(London: Collins 1973), vol.2.*

NICOLSON, Harold
Diaries and letters, 1939—45 *(London: Collins 1967)*, *512p.*

(POWNALL, *Sir* Henry) BOND, Brian *ed.*
Chief of Staff: the diaries of Lt. General Sir Henry Pownall, vol.2 1940—44 *(London: Cooper 1974), 216p.*

TAYLOR, Maxwell D
Swords and ploughshares *(New York: Norton 1972)*, *434p.*

WOOD, E F L *1st earl of Halifax*
Fullness of days *(London: Collins 1957), 319p.*

ZUCKERMAN, *Sir* Solly
From apes to warlords, 1904—1946 *(London: Hamilton 1978), 447p.*

MERCHANT NAVY

COWDEN, James E
The price of peace: Elder Dempster, 1939—1945 *(Liverpool: Jocart 1981), 99p.*

DONAHUE, Joseph A
Tin cans and other ships: a war diary, 1941—1945 *(North Quincey, Mass: Christopher 1979), 255p.*

HAY, Doddy
War under the Red Ensign: the Merchant Navy, 1939—45 *(London: Jane's 1982), 175p.*

MIDDLE EAST

ROBINSON, H R
Auchinleck to Alexander *(London: Hutchinson 1943)*, *196p.*
Wavell in the Middle East *(London: Hutchinson 1942)*, *236p.*

MIDWAY

FRANK, P *and* HARRINGTON, J
Rendezvous at Midway: USS Yorktown and the Japanese Carrier Fleet *(New York: Day 1967), 252p.*

SMITH, Peter C
The battle of Midway *(London: New English Library 1976), 189p.*

SMITH, William Ward
Midway: turning point of the Pacific *(New York: Crowell 1966), 174p.*

TAYLOR, Theodore
The battle of Midway Island *(New York: Avon 1981), 141p.*

[*see also PACIFIC, US MARINES, US NAVY*]

MINES AND MINESWEEPING

ELLIOTT, Peter
Allied minesweeping *(Cambridge: Stephens 1979), 201p.*

HARDY, Hilbert
The minesweeper's victory *(Weybridge, Sy: Eyot House 1976), 234p.*

LENTON, Henry T
American gunboats and minesweepers *(London: Macdonald & Jane's 1974), 64p.*

LUND, Paul
Out sweeps!: the story of the minesweepers in World War II *(London: Foulsham 1978), 192p.*

MOHNE DAM

COOPER, Alan W
The men who breached the dams *(London: Kimber 1982), 223p.*

SWEETMAN, John
Operation Cheshire: the dams raid: epic or myth *(London: Jane's 1982), 218p., bib.*

MONTGOMERY

CHALFONT, Alun J *1st baron*
Montgomery of Alamein *(London: Weidenfeld & Nicolson 1976), 365p.*

HAMILTON, Nigel
Monty: master of the battlefield, 1942—1944 *(London: Hamilton 1983), 863p., bib.*

LAMB, Richard
Montgomery in Europe, 1943—45 *(London: Buchan & Enright 1983), 416p.*

[*see also BRITISH ARMY (EIGHTH ARMY)(21st ARMY GROUP), EL ALAMEIN, NORMANDY, WESTERN EUROPE 1944—45*]

MOSQUITO

BOWYER, Michael
Mosquito *(London: Faber 1967), 494p.*

CURRIE, Jack
Mosquito victory *(London: Goodall 1983), 174p.*

HARDY, M J
The De Havilland Mosquito *(Newton Abbot, Devon: David & Charles 1977), 128p.*

MASON, F K
De Havilland Mosquito in RAF, FAA, RAAF, SAAF, RNZAF, USAAF and foreign service *(Canterbury, Kent: Osprey 1972), vol.I.*

TANNER, J *ed.*
The Mosquito manual: the official air publication for the Mosquito F MkII, NF Mark XII, and NF Mark XVIII, 1941—1945 *(London: Arms & Armour 1977), 300p.*

MOTOR TORPEDO BOATS

COOK, Graeme
Small boat raiders *(London: Hart-Davis, Macgibbon 1977)*,
130p., bib.

JOHNSON, Frank
United States P.T. boats of World War II in action *(Poole,
Dorset: Blandford 1980), 160p.*

NAGASAKI [see ATOM BOMB]

NAVAL WARFARE (general)

BAILEY, Thomas A *and* RYAN, P B
Hitler vs Roosevelt: the undeclared Naval war *(New York:
Macmillan 1979), 303p.*

BATCHELOR, John
Fighting ships of World War One and Two *(London:
Phoebus 1976), 255p.*

BECTON, F Julian *and* MORSCHAUSER, Joseph
The ship that would not die *(New York: Prentice-Hall
1980), 288p.*

BENNETT, Geoffrey
Naval battles of World War II *(London: Batsford 1975),
253p.*

CHAMBERS, Aidan *comp.*
War at sea *(London: Macmillan 1978), 119p.*

HAMPSHIRE, Arthur Cecil
The secret navies *(London: Kimber 1978), 272p., bib.*

LENTON, H T *and* COLLEDGE, J J
Warships of World War II *(London: Ian Allan 1964), 638p.*

LYON, David
World War II warships *(London: Orbis 1976), 127p.*

MILLER, Nathan
The naval air war, 1939—1945 *(London: Conway Maritime 1980), 224p.*

PACK, Stanley W C
The battle of Sirte *(London: Ian Allan 1975), 144p., bib.*

PRESTON, Antony
An illustrated history of the navies of World War II *(London: Hamlyn 1976), 224p.*

SMITH, Peter C
Action imminent: three studies of the naval war in the Mediterranean theatre during 1940 *(London: Kimber 1980), 352p.*

TOMLINSON, Michael
The most dangerous moment *(St Albans, Herts: Mayflower 1979), 221p.*

TURNER, L C F *and others*
War in the Southern Oceans, 1939—1945 *(London: OUP 1961), 288p., bib.*

WESTWOOD, John N
Fighting ships of World War II *(London: Sidgwick & Jackson 1975), 160p.*

WINTON, John
Air power at sea, 1939—45 *(London: Sidgwick & Jackson 1976), 185p., bib.*

[*see also NAVIES OF INDIVIDUAL COUNTRIES*]

NEGROES

DOWNLEY, Bill
Uncle Sam must be losing the war: black Marines of 51st *(San Francisco, Cal: Strawberry Hill 1982), 217p.*

FINKLE, Lee
Forum for protest: the Black Press during World War II *(Cranbury, NJ: Associated Universities 1975), 249p.*

MacGREGOR, Morris J *and* NALTY, Bernard
Blacks in the United States Armed Forces: vol. 5: Black soldiers in World War II *(Wilmington, Del: Scholarly Research)*, 521p.

McGUIRE, Phillip
Taps for a Jim Crow army: letters from black soldiers in World War II *(Santa Barbara, Cal: ABC—Clio 1983)*, 278p.

OSUR, Alan M
Blacks in the Army Air Forces during World War II *(New York: Arno 1980)*, 227p.

WYNN, Neil A
The Afro-American in the Second World War *(New York: Holmes & Meier 1976)*, 183p.

NETHERLANDS [see HOLLAND]

NEW GUINEA

MAYO, Lida
Bloody Buna: the campaign that halted the Japanese invasion of Australia *(London: New English Library 1977)*, 191p.

PARK, Edwards
Nanette *(New York: Norton 1977)*, 186p.

PAULL, Raymond
Retreat from Kokada: Australian campaign in New Guinea *(London: Cooper & Secker & Warburg 1983)*

ROBINSON, Neville K
Villagers at war: some New Guinean experiences in World War II *(Canberra, Aust: Australian National UP 1979)*, 223p.

NEW ZEALAND

ANDERSON, Peter N
Mustangs of the RAAF and RNZAF *(Sydney, Aust: Reed 1975), 103p., bib.*

DAVIN, Daniel M
Official history of New Zealand in the 2nd World War, 1939—1945 *(New Zealand War History Branch 1953)*

HENDERSON, J
22nd Battalion *(Wellington, NZ: Dept of Internal Affairs 1958)*

PUTTICK, E
History of the 25th Battalion *(Wellington, NZ: Dept of Internal Affairs 1960)*

VADER, J
Anzac *(London: New English Library 1970), 127p.*

NEW ZEALAND NAVY

HARKER, Jack S
HMNZS Achilles *(London: Collins 1980), 264p., bib.*

NIMITZ

POTTER, E B
Nimitz *(Annapolis, Md: Naval Institute 1976), 507p.*

NORMANDY

BELCHEM, David
Victory in Normandy *(London: Chatto & Windus 1981), 192p., bib.*

BENNETT, Ralph
Ultra in the West: the Normandy campaign of 1944—45 *(London: Hutchinson 1979), 305p.*

BLUMENSON, Martin
Liberation *(Alexandria, Va: Time-Life 1978), 208p.*

BOTTING, Douglas S
The Second Front *(Alexandria, Va: Time-Life 1978), 208p.*

BRUCE, George L
Second Front now: the road to D-Day *(London: Macdonald & Jane's 1979), 193p.*

CROOKENDEN, Napier
Dropzone Normandy: the story of the American and British airborne assault on D Day 1944 *(New York: Scribner 1976), 304p.*

D'ESTE, Carlo
Decision in Normandy: the unwritten story of Montgomery and the Allied campaign *(London: Collins 1983), 555p., bib.*

DUBOSCQ, Genevieve
My longest night *(New York: Seaver 1981), 284p.*

GILCHRIST, Donald
Don't cry for me: the Commandos D-Day and after *(London: Hale 1982), 192p.*

HARTCUP, Guy
Code name Mulberry: the planning, building and operation of the Normandy harbours *(Newton Abbot, Devon: David & Charles 1977), 160p., bib.*

HOW, J J
Normandy: the British breakout *(London: Kimber 1981), 238p., bib.*

HUNT, Robert
The Normandy campaign (camera at war) *(London: Cooper 1976)*

JACKSON, William G F
Overlord, Normandy 1944 *(London: Davis-Poynter 1978), 250p.*

JOHNSON, Garry *and* DUNPHIE, Christopher
Brightly shone the dawn: some experiences of the invasion of Normandy *(London: Warne 1980), 143p.*

KEEGAN, John
Six armies in Normandy *(London: Cape 1982), 365p., bib.*

LANE, Ronald L
Rudder's Rangers *(Manassas, Va: Ranger Associates 1979), unp.*

MAULE, Henry
Caen: the brutal battle and the break-out from Normandy *(Newton Abbot, Devon: David & Charles 1977), 160p.*

NORTH, John
North-West Europe, 1944–45: the achievement of 21st Army Group *(London: HMSO 1953), 270p.*

SWEET, John J T
Mounting the threat: the battle of Bourguebus Ridge 18–23 July 1944 *(Novato, Cal: Presidio 1978), 142p.*

WILT, Alan F
The Atlantic Wall: Hitler's defences in the West, 1941–1944 *(Ames, Iowa: Iowa State UP 1975), 244p.*

[*see also CAEN, D-DAY*]

NORTH AFRICA

BELCHEM, David
All in the day's march *(London: Collins 1978), 320p., bib.*

BLAXLAND, Gregory
The plain cook and the great showman: the First and Eighth Armies in North Africa *(London: Kimber 1977), 303p.*

BLUMENSON, Martin
Kasserine Pass *(Boston, Mass: Houghton, Mifflin 1967),
341p.*
UK title: Rommel's last victory

BOWYER, Chaz *and* SHORES, Christopher
Desert Air Force at war *(London: Ian Allan 1981), 128p.,
bib.*

BROWNLOW, Donald G
Checkmate at Ruiveisat: Auchinlek's finest hour *(North
Quincey, Mass: Christopher 1977), 209p.*

CHAPPELL, F R
Wellington wings: an RAF Intelligence Officer in the
Western Desert *(London: Kimber 1980), 282p.*

COGGINS, Jack
The campaign in North Africa *(New York: Doubleday
1980), 208p.*

COLLIER, Robert
The war in the desert *(Alexandria, Va: Time-Life 1978),
208p.*

COON, Carleton S
A North Africa story: the anthropologist as OSS agent,
1941—1943 *(Ipswich, Mass: Gambit 1980), 146p.*

FORTY, George
Desert Rats at war: North Africa *(London: Ian Allan
1975), 192p.*

HORSFALL, John
The wild geese are fighting *(Kineton, War: Roundwood
1976), 182p.*

JACKSON, Robert
Target Tobruk: yeoman of the Western Desert *(London:
Barker 1979), 167p.*

JACKSON, William G F
The battle for North Africa, 1940—43 *(New York: Mason-
Charles 1975), 393p., bib.*
UK title: The North Africa campaign

LLOYD OWEN, D L
Providence their guide: a personal account of the Long Range Desert Group, 1940—1945 *(London: Harrap 1980)*, *238p.*

MESSENGER, Charles
The Tunisian campaign *(London: Ian Allan 1982)*, *128p.*, *bib.*

PACK, Stanley W C
Invasion North Africa, 1942 *(London: Ian Allan 1978)*, *112p.*

PARKINSON, Roger
The war in the desert *(London: Hart-Davis 1976)*, *200p.*, *bib.*

PERRETT, Bryan *comp.*
Wavell's offensive *(London: Ian Allan 1979)*, *96p.*

PITT, Barrie
The crucible of war: Western Desert, 1941 *(London: Cape 1980)*, *506p.*

SAINSBURY, Keith
The North African landings, 1942: a strategic decision *(London: Davis-Poynter 1976)*, *215p.*, *bib.*

SANDARS, John
8th Army in the desert *(Cambridge: Stephens 1976)*, *64p.*
Operation Crusader *(London: Almark 1976)*, *48p.*

TUTE, Warren
The North African war *(London: Sidgwick & Jackson 1976)*, *222p.*

WARDROP, Jake
Tanks across the desert *(London: Kimber 1981)*, *22p.*, *bib.*

WILKINSON-LATHAM, John
Montgomery's desert Army *(London: Osprey 1977)*, *40p.*

[see also AFRIKA KORPS, BRITISH ARMY, RAF, US ARMY]

NORTH ATLANTIC

COSTELLO, John *and* HUGHES, Terry
The battle of the Atlantic *(London: Collins 1977), 314p., bib.*

POOLMAN, Kenneth
The sea hunters *(London: Arms & Armour 1982), 208p.*

NORWAY

GJELAVIK, Tore
Norwegian resistance, 1940—1945 *(London: Hurst & Blackett 1979), 224p.*

MILWARD, A S
The Fascist economy in Norway *(Oxford: Clarendon 1976), 317p., bib.*

NUREMBERG (AIR RAID ON)

TAYLOR, Geoffrey
The Nuremberg massacre *(London: Sidgwick & Jackson 1980), 176p.*

NURSES AND NURSING

BOYS, Doreen
Once upon a ward: V.A.D.'s own stories and pictures of service at home and overseas, 1939—1946 *(Upminster, Essex: Boys 1980), 207p.*

LONG, Helen
Change into uniform *(London: Gollancz 1978), 158p.*

McBRYDE, Brenda
A nurse's war *(London: Chatto & Windus 1979), 192p.*

RATLEDGE, Abbie C
Angels in khaki *(San Antonio, Tex: Naylor 1975), 182p.*

RODRIGUEZ, Helen
Helen of Burma *(London: Collins 1983), 192p.*

OSS (OFFICE OF STRATEGIC SERVICES)

CAVE BROWN, R *ed.*
The secret war report of the OSS *(New York: Berkeley 1976), 572p.*

HYMOFF, Edward
The OSS in World War II *(New York: Ballantine 1972), unp.*

SMITH, Bradley F
The shadow warriors: the OSS and the origins of the C.I.A. *(New York: Basic 1983), 507p.*

SMITH, Richard Harris
OSS: the secret history of America's first Central Intelligence Agency *(Berkeley, Cal: University of California 1972), 458p.*

OKINAWA

FRANK, B M
Okinawa: the great island battle *(New York: Dutton 1978), 184p.*

NICHOLS, C S *and* SHAW, H I
Okinawa: victory in the Pacific *(Rutland, Ver: Tuttle 1966), 332p.*

SLEDGE, Eugene B
With the old breed: at Peleliu and Okinawa *(Novato, Cal: Presidio 1981), 326p.*

[see also US MARINE CORPS]

ORIGINS

ADAMTHWAITE, Anthony
The making of the Second World War *(London: Allen & Unwin 1977), 240p., bib.*

BAUMONT, Maurice
The origins of the Second World War *(New Haven, Conn: Yale UP 1978), 327p.*

BLOOMBERG, Marty *and* WEBER, H H
World War II and its origins: a selected annotated bibliography of books in English *(Littleton, Cal: Libraries Unlimited 1975), 311p.*

CALVOCORESSI, Peter *and* WINT, G
Total war: causes and courses of the Second World War *(London: Penguin 1974), 965p.*

GANTENBEIN, James W *ed.*
Documentary background of World War II, 1931–1941 *(New York: Farrar Straus 1975), 1122p.*

KAISER, David E ·
Economic diplomacy and the origins of the Second World War *(Princeton, NJ: Princeton UP 1980), 346p., bib.*

OFFNER, Arnold A
The origins of the Second World War: American foreign policy and world politics, 1917–1941 *(New York: Praeger 1975), 268p.*

OVENDALL, Ritchie
Appeasement and the English speaking world: Britain, the U.S., the Dominions and the policy of appeasement, 1937–1939 *(Cardiff, Wales: University of Wales 1975), 358p.*

REMAK, Joachim *comp.*
The origins of the Second World War *(London: Prentice-Hall 1976), 179p.*

SALLAGAR, Frederick M
The road to total war *(New York: Van Nostrand 1975), 197p., bib.*

WATT, Donald C
Too serious a business: European Armed Forces and the approach to the Second World War *(Berkeley, Cal: University of California 1975), 200p.*

PACIFIC

ADAMS, Bruce
Rust in peace: South Pacific battlegrounds revisited *(Artarmon, Aust: Antipodean 1976), 239p.*

BAILEY, Dan E
World War II wrecks of the Kwajalein and Truk lagoons *(Redding, Cal: North Valley Diver 1982), 144p.*

BRONEMANN, Leroy C
Once upon a tide: tales from a foxhole in the South Pacific *(New York: Dorrance 1982), 185p.*

COSTELLO, John
The Pacific war *(London: Collins 1981), 242p., bib.*

HILDER, Brett
Navigator in the South Seas *(London: Marshall 1961), 232p.*

HOYT, Edwin P
Closing the circle: war in the Pacific, 1945 *(New York: Van Nostrand 1982), 240p.*
Storm over the Gilberts: war in the Central Pacific *(New York: Van Nostrand 1978), 175p.*
To the Marianas: war in the Central Pacific, 1944 *(New York: Reinhold 1980), 292p., bib.*

IENAGA, Saburo
The Pacific war: World War II and the Japanese, 1931–1945 *(New York: Random House 1978), 316p.*
UK title: Japan's last war

LINDLEY, John M
Carrier victory: the air war in the Pacific *(New York: Dutton 1978), 184p.*

LUNDSTROM, John B
The first South Pacific campaign: Pacific Fleet strategy, December 1941—June 1942 *(Annapolis, Md: Naval Institute 1976), 240p.*

MANCHESTER, William R
Goodbye darkness: a memoir of the Pacific war *(Boston, Mass: Little, Brown 1980), 401p.*

MORRISON, Wilbur H
Above and beyond, 1941—1945 *(New York: St Martin's 1983), 314p.*

PRESTON, Anthony *ed.*
Decisive battles of the Pacific war *(London: Bison 1979), 180p.*

REESE, Lee F *comp.*
Men of the blue ghost: USS Lexington CV-16, historical events of World War II in the Pacific *(San Diego, Cal: Lexington 1980), 923p.*

ROSENBERG, Philip A
Shipwrecks of Truk *(Kealakekua, Hawaii: Par Photo 1981), 102p.*

SOWINSKI, Larry
The Pacific war: as seen by US Navy photographers during World War Two *(London: Conway Maritime 1981), 208p.*

STEINBERG, Rafael *ed.*
World War II: island fighting *(Alexandria, Va: Time-Life 1978), 208p.*

TRUMBULL, Robert
Tin roofs and palm trees *(Seattle, Wash: University of Washington 1977), 302p.*

TUPOUNIUA, Sione *and others*
The Pacific way *(Suva, Fiji 1975)*

VADER, John
Pacific hawk *(London: Macdonald 1970), 160p.*

WAR In Asia and the Pacific, 1937—1949 *(New York: Garland 1980), 15 vols*

WELSH, Douglas
The U.S.A. in World War Two: the Pacific theater *(New York: Garland 1982), 64p.*

WHITEHOUSE, Arch
Heroes of the sunlit sky *(New York: Doubleday 1967), 384p.*

WINTON, John
War in the Pacific: Pearl Harbor to Tokyo Bay *(London: Sidgwick & Jackson 1978), 193p.*

[*see also US MARINE CORPS, US NAVY*]

PACIFISM [see CONSCIENTIOUS OBJECTORS]

PARACHUTISTS [see AIRBORNE FORCES]

PARIS

PRYCE-JONES, David
Paris in the Third Reich: a history of the German occupation 1940—1944 *(London: Collins 1981), 294p.*

PARTISANS [see RESISTANCE]

PATHFINDERS

BOWYER, Chaz
Pathfinders at war *(London: Ian Allan 1977), 160p.*

MUSGROVE, Gordon
Pathfinder force: a history of 8 Group *(London: Macdonald & Jane's 1976), 302p.*

PATTON

BLUMENSON, Martin
The Patton papers, 1940—1945 *(Boston, Mass: Houghton-Mifflin 1974), 2 vols*

FARAGO, Ladislas
The last days of Patton *(New York: McGraw Hill 1981), 391p.*

WELLARD, James H
General George S. Patton, jun.: man under Mars *(New York: Dodd 1946)*
UK title: The man in a helmet

PEACE

ROSTOW, W W
The division of Europe after World War II, 1946 *(Aldershot, Hants: Gower 1982), 212p.*

WARD, Patricia D
The threat of peace: James F. Byrnes and the Council of Foreign Ministers, 1945—1946 *(Kent, Ohio: Kent State UP 1979), 227p.*

PEARL HARBOR

BARTLETT, B R
Cover-up: the politics of Pearl Harbor, 1941—46 *(New York: Arlington 1978), 189p.*

BORG, D *ed.*
Pearl Harbor as history *(New York: Columbia UP 1973), 801p.*

BROWNLOW, Donald G
The accused: the ordeal of Rear Admiral Husband Edward Kimmel USN *(New York: Vantage 1968), 190p.*

COLLIER, Richard
The road to Pearl Harbor 1941 *(New York: Atheneum 1981), 310p.*

MELOSI, Martin V
The shadow of Pearl Harbor: political controversies over the surprise attack, 1941—1946 *(College Station, Tex: Texas A & M UP 1977), 183p.*

PRANGE, Gordon W
At dawn we slept: the untold story of Pearl Harbor *(London: Joseph 1982), 873p., bib.*

STRATTON, Roy
The Army—Navy game *(Falmouth, Ma: Volta 1977)*

TOLAND, John
Infamy: Pearl Harbor and its aftermath *(London: Methuen 1982), 366p., bib.*

PEENEMUNDE

MIDDLEBROOK, Martin
The Peenemunde raid: the night of 17—18 August 1943 *(London: Ian Allan 1982), 256p., bib.*

PERSONAL NARRATIVE

BEAUMAN, Archibald B
Then a soldier *(London: Macmillan 1960), 186p.*

BROWN, Walter L
Up front with the U.S. *(Oakland, Cal: Author 1980), 744p.*

COOPER, Miles
Last on the list *(London: Cooper 1974), 228p.*

DOWNING, John P
At war with the British *(Daytona Beach, Fla: Downing 1980), 204p.*

DUMAIS, Lucien *and* POPHAM, Hugh
The man who went back *(London: Futura 1975), 213p.*

ECCLES, David *1st viscount*
By safe hand: the wartime letters of David and Sybil
Eccles *(London: Bodley Head 1982), 384p.*

GALVIN, John
Salvation for a doomed zoomie *(Indian Hills, Col: Allnutt
1983), 272p.*

GLEN, Alexander
Footholds against a whirlwind *(London: Hutchinson
1975), 275p.*

GOLD, Mary J
Crossroads Marseilles 1940 *(New York: Doubleday 1980),
412p.*

HARVEY, John *ed.*
The war diaries of Oliver Harvey, 1941—1945 *(London:
Collins 1978), 399p.*

HERNDON, James
Sorrowless times: a narrative *(New York: Simon & Schuster
1981), 185p.*

HOUGH, Richard A
One boy's war *(London: Heinemann 1975), 151p.*

JONES, Francis S T
The double-Dutchman *(London: Corgi 1978), 189p.*

JONES, Tristan
Heart of oak *(London: Bodley Head 1983), 256p.*

KELLY, Arthur J
There's a goddam bullet for everyone *(Paris, Ontario:
Tyoweronh 1979), 331p.*

KREYE, William M
The pawns of war *(New York: Vantage 1983), 284p.*

LIDZ, Richard
Many kinds of courage: an oral history of World War II
(New York: Putnam 1980), 206p.

MILBURN, Clara E
Mrs. Milburn's diaries: an English-woman's day-to-day
reflections, 1939—1945 *(London: Harrap 1979), 364p.*

MILLAR, George R
Road to resistance: an autobiography *(London: Bodley Head 1979), 411p.*

MONSARRAT, Nicholas
Monsarrat at sea *(New York: Morrow 1976), 342p.*

MOWAT, Farley M
And no birds sang *(Boston, Mass: Little, Brown 1980), 219p.*

POLLOCK, P H
Wings on the Cross *(New York: Exposition 1978), 223p.*

ROCHESTER, Devereux
Full moon to France *(New York: Harper 1977), 261p.*

ROUBICZEK, Paul
Across the abyss: diary entries for the year 1939—1940 *(Cambridge: CUP 1982), 325p.*

ST ALBANS, Suzanne A *duchess of*
Uncertain wings *(London: W.H. Allen 1977), 216p.*

STOVER, Elisha T *and* REYNOLDS, C G
The saga of Smokey Stover *(Charleston, SC: Tradd Street 1978), 119p.*

TAYLOR, F A J
The bottom of the barrel *(London: Regency 1978), 174p.*

TOLLEY, Kemp
Cruise of the Lanikai: incitement to war *(Melbourne, Fla: Krieger 1982), 345p.*

VINING, Donald *ed.*
American diaries of World War II *(New York: Pepys 1982), 430p.*

WINDSOR, John B
The mouth of the wolf *(Toronto: Collins 1978), 223p.*

PHILIPPINES

DICKSON, William D
The battle of the Philippine Sea, June 1944 *(London: Ian Allan 1975), 256p.*

JOHNSON, Forrest B
Hour of redemption: the Ranger raid on Cabanatuan *(New York: Manor 1978), 395p.*

NETZORG, Morton J
The Philippines in World War II, and to independence (December 8, 1941—July 4, 1946: an annotated bibliography) *(Ithaca, NY: Cornell UP 1977), 232p.*

PRISING, Robert
Manila, goodbye *(Boston, Mass: Houghton-Mifflin 1975), 207p.*

QUEZON, Michael L
The good fight *(New York: AMS 1974), 335p.*

ROMULO, Carlos P
I see the Philippines rise *(New York: AMS 1975), 273p.*

STEINBERG, Rafael
Return to the Philippines *(Alexandria, Va: Time-Life 1979), 208p.*
UK title: Island fighting

WILLOUGHBY, Charles A
The guerrilla resistance in the Philippines *(New York: Vantage 1972), 702p.*

PHOTOGRAPHY

BEATON, Cecil
War photographs, 1939—45 *(London: Jane's 1981), 189p.*

BROOKES, Andrew J
Photo-reconnaissance *(London: Ian Allan 1975), 247p.*

CAMERA At sea, 1939—45 *(London: Conway Maritime 1978), 192p.*

COLLIER, Basil
Japan at war: an illustrated history of the war in the Far
East, 1931—1945 *(London: Sidgwick & Jackson 1975),
192p.*

DOLLINGER, Hans
The decline and fall of Nazi Germany and Imperial Japan:
a picture history of the final days of World War II *(New
York: Bonanza 1982), 431p.*

GRANT, Ian
Cameraman at war *(Cambridge: Stephens 1980), 102p.*

HERRIDGE, Charles
Pictorial history of World War II *(London: Hamlyn 1975),
253p.*

HOOBLER, Dorothy *and* HOOBLER, Thomas
An album of World War II *(London: Watts 1977), 66p.*

JABLONSKI, Edward
A pictorial history of the World War II years *(New York:
Doubleday 1977), 319p.*

LIFE Goes to war: a picture history of World War II *(Boston,
Mass: Little, Brown 1977), 303p.*

MAYER, Sidney L
Pictorial history of World War II *(London: Octopus 1976),
128p.*

MOLLO, Andrew *comp.*
A pictorial history of the SS, 1923—1945 *(London:
Macdonald & Jane's 1976), 192p., bib.*

PHILLIPS, Christopher
Steichen at war *(New York: Abrams 1981), 256p.*

QUARRIE, Bruce *comp.*
Waffen SS in Russia: selection of German wartime photos
(Cambridge: Stephens 1978), 95p.

SWASTIKA At war: a photographic record of the war as seen
by the cameramen of the German magazine Signal *(New
York: Doubleday 1975), unp.*

WORLD War 2 photo album *(Cambridge: Stephens), 6 vols*

PLYMOUTH

WINTLE, Frank
The Plymouth blitz *(Bodmin, Cornwall: Bossiney 1981)*, *96p., bib.*

POLAND

BIDDLE, Anthony J D
Poland and the coming of the Second World War: the diplomatic papers of H.J. Drexel, *jun.* U.S. Ambassador to Poland, 1937—39 *(Columbus, Ohio: Ohio State UP 1976)*, *358p.*

CENTRAL COMMISSION FOR INVESTIGATION OF GERMAN CRIMES IN POLAND
German crimes in Poland *(New York: Fertig 1982)*, *168p.*

DONAT, Alexander
The holocaust kingdom *(New York: Holt 1965)*, *362p.*

GROSS, Jan T
Poland under German occupation: the General Government, 1939—1944 *(Guildford, Sy: UP of Columbia and Princeton 1979)*, *343p.*

HEIT, Edmund *and* HEIT, C
The Soviets are coming *(New York: Gospel 1980)*, *159p.*

KACEWICZ, George V
Great Britain, the Soviet Union and the Polish Government in exile, 1939—1945 *(London: Nijhoff 1979)*, *255p., bib.*

KOMOROWSKI, Eugenfusz A *and* GILMORE, J L
Night never ending *(New York: Avon 1975)*, *285p.*

KORBONSKI, Stefan
The Polish underground state: a guide to the underground, 1939—1945 *(New York: Columbia UP 1978)*, *268p.*

NOWAK, Jan
Courier from Warsaw *(London: Collins 1982)*, *477p.*

PIASECKI, Victor
You'll need a guardian angel *(London: Hamilton 1979)*, *208p.*

POLONSKY, Antony *ed.*
The great powers and the Polish question, 1941—1945 *(London: Orbis 1976), 282p.*

RASCHKE, Jan
Farewell to God *(Dundee, Scot: Wright 1977), 207p.*

TERRY, Sarah M
Poland's place in Europe: General Sikorski and the origins of the Oder-Neisse line, 1939—1943 *(Princeton, NJ: Princeton UP 1983), 394p.*

[*see also CONCENTRATION CAMPS, JEWS, WARSAW*]

POLITICS

ADDISON, Paul
The road to 1945: British politics and the Second World War *(London: Cape 1975), 334p., bib.*

BURRIDGE, Trevor D
British Labour and Hitler's war *(London: Deutsch 1976), 206p., bib.*

NICHOLAS, Herbert G *ed.*
Washington despatches, 1941—1945; weekly political reports from the British Embassy *(Chicago, Ill: Chicago UP 1981), 700p.*

PORTAL

RICHARDS, Denis
Portal of Hungerford: the life of Marshal of the Royal Air Force Viscount Portal of Hungerford *(London: Heinemann 1978), 436p.*

POTSDAM

FEIS, Herbert
Between war and peace: the Potsdam Conference *(London: OUP 1960), 367p.*

MEE, Charles L
Meeting at Potsdam *(London: Deutsch 1975), 370p.*

PRESS

ANGLO, M
Service newspapers of the Second World War *(London: Jupiter 1977), 138p.*

BUDD, Edward
A printer goes to war *(London: Howard Baker 1975), 182p.*

THE WAR Despatches, 1939—1945 *(London: Cavendish 1977), 160p.*

PRISONER OF WAR CAMPS

BEESON, George
Five roads to Dresden *(London: Corgi 1978), 144p.*

BORRIE, John
Despite captivity *(London: Kimber 1975), 240p.*

BROWN, John
In durance vile *(London: Hale 1981), 160p., bib.*

BROWN, Stuart
Forbidden paths *(Edinburgh: Harris 1978), 170p.*

EDGAR, Donald
The Stalag Men *(London: Clare 1982), 192p.*

FAULK, Henry
Group captives: the re-education of German prisoners of war *(London: Chatto & Windus 1977), 233p.*

FENELON, Fania *and* ROUTIER, M
Playing for time *(New York: Berkeley 1979), 289p.*

GANSBERG, Judith M
Stalag U.S.A.: the remarkable story of German POW's in America *(New York: Crowell 1977), 233p.*

HEIMLER, Eugene
Night of the mist *(Westport, Conn: Greenwood 1978), 191p.*

KEE, Robert
A crowd is not company *(London: Cape 1982), 2nd ed. 256p.*

KOCHAN, Miriam
Prisoners of England *(London: Macmillan 1980), 254p., bib.*

LACAZE, Andre
The tunnel *(London: Hamilton 1980), 416p.*

LARIVE, Etienne H
The man who came in from Colditz *(London: Hale 1975), 192p.*

LOVELL, Terry
Camera in Colditz *(London: Hodder & Stoughton 1982), 160p.*

McCANN, Hugh R *and others*
The search for Johnny Nicholas *(London: Sphere 1982), 369p.*

MACKAY, Alan
Barbed wire and blue pencil *(Edinburgh: Polygon 1983)*

MANSEL, John
The Mansel diaries: the diaries of Captain John Mansel, P.O.W., and camp forger in Germany, 1940–45 *(London: Wildwood House 1977), 156p.*

OGILVIE, Peter
In the bag *(Johannesburg: Macmillan 1975), 101p.*

PARNELL, Wilma T
The death of Corporal Kunze *(Secaucus, NJ: Stuart 1981), 168p.*

PLATT, J Ellison
Padre in Colditz *(London: Hodder & Stoughton 1980),*
320p.

REID, Miles
Into Colditz *(Salisbury, Wilts: Russell 1983), 95p.*

SULLIVAN, Barry
Thresholds of peace: four hundred thousand German
prisoners and the people of Britain *(London: Hamilton
1979), 420p., bib.*

THROWER, Derek
The lonely path to freedom *(London: Hale 1980), 159p.*

PROPAGANDA

BAIRD, Jay W
The mythical world of Nazi war propaganda, 1939—1945
(Minneapolis: University of Minnesota 1975), 329p.

BALFOUR, Michael L G
Propaganda in war, 1939—1945: organizations, policies
and publics in Britain and Germany *(London: Routledge
& Kegan Paul 1979), 520p., bib.*

BOYLE, Andrew
Poor dear Brendan *(London: Hutchinson 1974), 377p.*

HERZSTEIN, Robert C
The war that Hitler won: the most infamous propaganda
campaign in history *(New York: Putnam 1978), 491p.,
bib.*

HOWE, Ellis
The black game: British subversive operations against
Germans during the Second World War *(London: Joseph
1982), 276p.*

RHODES, Anthony R E
Propaganda: the art of persuasion: World War II *(New
York: Chelsea House 1976), 319p.*

RUPP, Leila J
Mobilizing women for war: German and American propaganda, 1939—1945 *(Princeton, NJ: Princeton UP 1978)*, *243p.*

SHORT, R M *ed.*
Film and radio propaganda in World War II *(London: Croom Helm 1983)*, *341p.*

SPROAT, Iain
Wodehouse at war *(New Haven, Conn: Ticknor & Fields 1981)*, *300p.*

TAYLOR, Richard
Film propaganda, Soviet Russia and Nazi Germany *(New York: Harper 1979)*, *265p.*

ZEMAN, Zbynek
Selling the war: art and propaganda in World War II *(London: Orbis 1978)*, *120p., bib.*

PSYCHOLOGY

CRUICKSHANK, Charles
The fourth arm: Psychological warfare, 1938—45 *(London: Davis-Poynton: 1977)*, *200p., bib.*

RICHARDSON, Frank
Fighting spirit: a study of psychological factors in war *(London: Cape 1978)*, *189p., bib.*

WATSON, Peter
War on the mind: military uses and abuses of psychology *(London: Hutchinson 1978)*, *534p.*

PURPLE

CLARK, Ronald W
The man who broke 'Purple': the life of the world's greatest cryptologist, William F. Friedman *(London: Weidenfeld & Nicolson 1977)*, *212p.*

LEWIN, Ronald
The American Magic: codes, ciphers and the defeat of Japan *(New York: Farrar 1982), 332p.*

[*see also MAGIC, ULTRA*]

RADAR

HILL, Robert
The great coup *(London: Arlington 1977), 172p.*

HOWARD-WILLIAMS, Jeremy N
Night intruder: a personal account of the radar war between the RAF and Luftwaffe night-fighter forces *(Newton Abbot, Devon: David & Charles 1976), 184p.*

PRICE, Alfred
Instruments of darkness: the history of electronic warfare *(London: Macdonald & Jane's 1977), 333p.*

RADIO

BRIGGS, Asa
The war of words *(London: OUP 1970), vol.3, 766p.*

REFERENCE BOOKS

KEEGAN, John
Who was Who in World War II *(London: Arms & Armour 1978), 224p.*

MASON, David
Who's Who in World War II *(London: Weidenfeld & Nicolson 1978), 367p.*

SNYDER, Louis L
Louis L. Snyder's historical guide to World War II *(Westport, Conn: Greenwood 1982), 838p.*

REFUGEES

GILLMAN, Peter
'Collar the lot': how Britain interned and expelled its war-time refugees *(London: Quartet 1980), 334p., bib.*

GRUBER, Ruth
Haven: the unknown story of 1000 World War II refugees *(New York: Coward-McCann 1983), 335p.*

KUNZ, Egon C
The intruders: refugee doctors in Australia *(Canberra: Australian National UP 1975), 139p.*

WOLF, Ingrid
With the help of Thomas *(London: Hale 1980), 206p.*

REPATRIATION

ELLIOTT, Mark R
Pawns of Yalta: Soviet refugees and America's role in their repatriation *(Champaign, Ill: University of Illinois 1982), 287p.*

TOLSTOY, Nikolai
Victims of Yalta *(London: Hodder & Stoughton 1977), 496p.*

RESISTANCE

BLUMENSON, Martin
The Vilde affair: beginnings of French resistance *(Boston, Mass: Houghton-Mifflin 1977), 287p.*

BRASON, John
The secret army *(London: BBC 1977), 176p.*

FOOT, Michael R D
Resistance: an analysis of European resistance to Nazism, 1940–1945 *(London: Eyre Methuen 1976), 346p., bib.*
Six faces of courage *(London: Eyre Methuen 1978), 134p., bib.*

FRENAY, Henri
The night will end *(New York: McGraw-Hill 1975), 469p.*

GOLDSTON, Robert C
Sinister touches: the secret war against Hitler *(New York: Dial 1982), 214p.*

HAWES, Stephen *and* WHITE, Ralph *eds*
Resistance in Europe, 1939—45: based on proceedings of a symposium held at the University of Salford, 1973 *(London: Lane 1975), 234p., bib.*

HEALEY, Tim
Secret armies: resistance groups in World War II *(London: Macdonald 1981), 48p.*

KNIGHT, Frida
The French resistance, 1940—1944 *(London: Lawrence & Wishart 1975), 242p.*

LIONEL, Frederic
Challenge: on special mission *(Sudbury, Sy: Spearman 1980), 147p.*

MACKSEY, Kenneth J
The partisans of Europe in the Second World War *(New York: Stein & Day 1975), 271p.*

MICHEL, Henri
Resistance in Europe, 1939—1945 *(London: Ian Allan 1975), 414p.*
Also published as: Shadow war

MILLER, Russell
The resistance *(Alexandria, Va: Time-Life 1979), 208p., bib.*

MOLDEN, Fritz
Exploding star: a young Austrian against Hitler *(New York: Morrow 1979), 280p.*

MOUNTFIELD, David
The partisans: secret armies of World War II *(London: Hamlyn 1979), 192p.*

ORTZEN, Len
Famous stories of the resistance *(London: Barker 1979),*
154p., bib.

SCHOENBRUN, David
Soldiers of the night: the story of the French resistance
(New York: Elsevier-Dutton 1980), 512p., bib.

WILKINSON, James D
The intellectual resistance in Europe *(Cambridge, Mass:*
Harvard UP 1983), 358p.

WOLF, Jacqueline
Take care of Josette: a memoir in defence of occupied
France *(New York: Watts 1981), 184p.*

[*see also INDIVIDUAL COUNTRIES, SOE*]

RIVIERA CAMPAIGN

LESLIE, Peter
The liberation of the Riviera: the resistance to the Nazis
in the south of France and the story of the heroic leader
Ange-Marie Miniconi *(New York: Simon & Schuster*
1980), 254p.

WILT, Alan F
The French Riviera campaign of August 1944 *(Carbondale,*
Ill: Southern Illinois UP 1981), 208p.

ROME

KURZMAN, Dan
The race for Rome *(New York: Doubleday 1975), 488p.*

TREVELYAN, Raleigh
Rome '44: the battle for the eternal city *(London: Secker*
& Warburg 1981), 364p.

ROMMEL

BLANCO, Richard L
Rommel, the desert warrior: the Afrika Korps in World War II *(New York: Messner 1982), 191p.*

HECKMAN, Wolf
Rommel's war in Africa *(London: Granada 1981), 366p., bib.*

IRVING, David
The trail of the Fox: the life of Field Marshal Erwin Rommel *(London: Weidenfeld & Nicolson 1977), 448p., bib.*

MACKSEY, Kenneth J
Rommel: battles and campaigns *(London: Arms & Armour 1979), 224p., bib.*

MITCHAM, Samuel W
Rommel's desert war: the life and death of the Afrika Korps *(New York: Stein & Day 1982), 219p.*

RUGE, Friedrich
Rommel in Normandy: reminiscences *(London: Macdonald & Jane's 1979), 266p.*

SCHMIDT, Heinz W
With Rommel in the desert *(London: Harrap 1980), 240p.*

[*see also AFRIKA KORPS, NORMANDY*]

ROOSEVELT

DALLEK, Robert *ed.*
The Roosevelt diplomacy and World War II *(Huntington, NY: Krieger 1978), 125p.*

FREIDEL, F
Franklin D. Roosevelt *(Boston: Little, Brown), 6 vols*

LASH, Joseph P
Roosevelt and Churchill, 1939—1941: the partnership that saved the West *(London: Deutsch 1977), 528p.*

LOEWENHEIM, F L *and others*
Roosevelt and Churchill: their secret wartime correspondence *(London: Barrie & Jenkins 1975), 807p.*

ROOSEVELT, Elliott *ed.*
The Roosevelt letters: the personal correspondence of F.D. Roosevelt, 1928—1945 *(London: Harrap 1952), vol.3, 541p.*

ROYAL AIR FORCE

ADKIN, F J
From the ground up: a history of R.A.F. ground crew *(Shrewsbury, Salop: Airlife 1983), 219p.*

BARKER, Ralph
The RAF at war *(Alexandria, Va: Time-Life 1981), 176p.*

BEAUMONT, Roland
Phoenix into ashes *(London: Kimber 1968), 192p.*

BOWYER, Michael
Aircraft for the Royal Air Force *(London: Faber 1980), 170p.*
2nd Group Royal Air Force: a complete history, 1926—1945 *(London: Faber 1979), 532p.*

CHORLEY, W R *and* BENWELL, R N
In brave company: the history of 158 Squadron *(Woking, Sy: Chorley 1978), 172p.*

COOKSLEY, Peter G
1940: the story of No.II Group Fighter Command *(London: Hale 1983), 224p.*

DEAN, *Sir* Maurice
The RAF and two world wars *(London: Cassell 1979), 368p.*

FAIRHEAD, R
An airman's diary *(Bognor Regis, Sx: New Horizon 1982), 103p.*

FOXLEY-NORRIS, *Sir* Christopher
Royal Air Force at war *(London: Ian Allan 1983), 144p.*

GODEFROY, Hugh C
Lucky thirteen *(London: Croom Helm 1983), 274p.*

HAUGHLAND, Vern
The Eagle Squadron: Yanks in the R.A.F., 1940—1942 *(New York: McGraw-Hill 1979), 206p.*

JACKSON, Robert
The secret squadrons *(London: Robson 1983), 192p.*

McCALL, Gibb
Flight most secret: air missions for SOE and SIS *(London: Kimber 1981), 270p., bib.*

McVICAR, Don
Ferry Command *(Shrewsbury, Salop: Airlife 1981), 213p.*

NESBIT, Roy C
Torpedo airmen: missions with Bristol Beauforts, 1940—42 *(London: Kimber 1983), 234p.*

RAPIER, Brian J
Melbourne ten *(York: Air Museum 1982), 164p.*

ROBERTSON, Bruce
Beaufort special *(London: Ian Allan 1976), 80p.*
Lysander special *(London: Ian Allan 1977), 64p.*

SAUNDERS, Hilary St G
Royal Air Force, 1943—1945 *(London: HMSO 1954), 3 vols*

TANNER, J *ed.*
British aviation colours of World War II *(London: Arms & Armour 1976), 64p.*

TURNER, John F
British aircraft of World War II, with colour photographs *(London: Sidgwick & Jackson 1975), 144p.*

WALLACE, Graham F
Guns of the RAF, 1939—1945 *(London: Kimber 1972), 221p.*

WINFIELD, Roland
The sky belongs to them *(London: Kimber 1976), 188p.*

ZIEGLER, Frank H
The story of 609 Squadron: under the White Rose *(London: Macdonald 1971), 352p.*

[*see also BOMBERS, FIGHTERS*]

ROYAL MARINES

DEAR, Ian
Marines at war *(London: Ian Allan 1982), 128p.*

[*see also COMMANDOS*]

ROYAL NAVY

AITKEN, Alex
In time of war *(Glasgow: Aitken 1980)*

BROOKE, Geoffrey
Alarm starboard: a remarkable true story of the war at sea *(Cambridge: Stephens 1982), 280p.*

HAMPSHIRE, A Cecil
Undercover sailors: secret operations in World War II *(London: Kimber 1981), 208p., bib.*

HARRISON, William A
Swordfish special *(London: Ian Allan 1977), 80p.*

HOLMES, David
Not beyond recall *(Bognor Regis, Sx: New Horizon 1982), 81p.*

JULLIAN, Marcel
HMS Fidelity *(London: Futura 1975), 176p.*

LENTON, Henry T
British escort ships *(New York: Arco 1975), 64p.*

LOMBARD-HOBSON, Sam
A sailor's war *(New York: St Martin's 1983), 174p.*

MARDER, Arthur
From the Dardanelles to Oran: studies of the Royal Navy in war and peace, 1915−1940 *(London: OUP 1974), 320p.*

SCHOFIELD, B B *and* MARTYN, L F
The rescue ships *(London: Blackwood 1968), 172p.*

TROMAN, L
Wine, women and war *(London: Regency 1979), 97p.*

WILLIAMS, Eve
Ladies without lamps *(London: Harmsworth 1983), 178p.*

WILLIAMS, Mark
Captain Gilbert Roberts, R.N., and the anti-U-boat school *(London: Cassell 1979), 186p.*

YOUNG, John
A dictionary of ships of the Royal Navy of the Second World War *(Cambridge: Stephens 1975), 192p.*

ROYAL OBSERVER CORPS

WOOD, Derek
Attack warning red: the Royal Observer Corps and the defence of Britain, 1925−1975 *(London: Macdonald & Jane's 1976), 357p.*

RUMANIA

NEWBY, Leroy W
Target Ploesti: view from a bombsight *(London: Arms & Armour 1983), 288p.*

RUSSIA

BETHELL, Nicholas W *4th baron*
Russia besieged *(Alexandria, Va: Time-Life 1977), 208p.*

BONDS, Ray *ed.*
The Soviet war machine: an encyclopaedia of Russian military equipment and strategy *(London: Hamlyn 1976), 247p.*

BRADLEY, John *and others*
The Russian war machine, 1917–1945 *(London: Arms & Armour 1977), 256p.*

CHANT, Christopher
Kursk *(London: Almark 1975), 480p.*

ERICKSON, John
Stalin's war with Germany: vol.I, the road to Stalingrad *(London: Weidenfeld & Nicolson 1975), 594p.*

KLEINFELD, Gerald R *and* TAMBS, L A
Hitler's Spanish Legion: the Blue Division in Russia *(Carbondale, Ill: Southern Illinois UP 1979), 434p.*

LYONS, Graham *ed.*
The Russian version of the Second World War: the history of the war as taught to Soviet schoolchildren *(London: Cooper 1976), 142p.*

MASTNY, Vojtech
Russia's road to the cold war: diplomacy, warfare and politics of Communism, 1941–45 *(Guildford, Sy: Columbia UP 1979), 409p.*

MYLES, Bruce
Night witches: the untold story of Soviet women in combat *(Edinburgh: Mainstream 1981), 278p.*

ZIEMKE, Earl F
The Soviet juggernaut *(Alexandria, Va: Time-Life 1980), 208p.*

RUSSIAN AIR FORCE

GREEN, William *and* SWANBOROUGH, F G
Soviet Air Force fighters *(London: Macdonald & Jane's 1977), 68p.*

HARDESTY, Von
Red phoenix: the rise of Soviet air power, 1941—1945 *(Washington DC: Smithsonian Institute 1982), 288p.*

RUSSIAN ARMY

BASANSKY, Bill *and* MANUEL, David
Babunia *(Plainfield, NJ: Logos 1976), 190p.*

SCRIABINE, Helene A
After Leningrad: from the Caucasus to the Rhine, Aug 9, 1942—Mar 25, 1945 *(New York: Feffer & Simons 1978), 190p.*

VITUKHIN, Igor *ed.*
Soviet Generals recall World War II *(New York: Sphinx 1981), 411p.*

RUSSIAN NAVY

ACHKASOV, V I *and* PAVLOVICH, N B
Soviet naval operations in the Great Patriotic War, 1941—1945 *(Annapolis, Md: Naval Institute 1981), 393p.*

RUGE, Friedrich
The Soviets as naval opponents, 1941—1945 *(Annapolis, Md: Naval Institute 1979), 210p.*

RUSSIAN PRISONS

CISNEK, Walter J *and* FLAHERTY, D L
He leadeth me *(New York: Doubleday 1975), 232p.*

RUPERT, R
A hidden world *(London: Collins 1963), 224p.*

SALERNO

HICKEY, Des
Operation Avalanche: the Salerno landings *(London: Heinemann 1983), 379p., bib.*

MORRIS, Eric
Salerno *(London: Hutchinson 1983), 358p.*

SCAPA FLOW

SNYDER, Gerald S
The 'Royal Oak' disaster *(London: Kimber 1976), 240p., bib.*

WEAVER, H J
Nightmare at Scapa Flow *(Henley-on-Thames, Oxon: Cressvelles 1980), 192p.*

SCHWEINFURT RAID

MIDDLEBROOK, Martin
The Schweinfurt-Regensburg mission: American raids on 17 August 1943 *(London: Lane 1983), 352p.*

SEA LION

LONGMATE, Norman
If Britain had fallen *(London: BBC 1975), 276p.*

MACKSEY, Kenneth
Invasion: the German invasion of England, July 1940 *(London: Arms & Armour 1980), 224p., bib.*

OPERATION Sea Lion *(London: Thornton Cox 1974), 190p.*
Also published as: Sea Lion

SECRET SERVICE

BANCROFT, Mary
Autobiography of a spy *(New York: Morrow 1983), 300p.*

BUTLER, Josephine
Churchill's secret agent *(London: Blaketon-Hall 1983), 205p.*

CAVE BROWN, Anthony
Bodyguard of lies *(New York: Harper 1975), 947p., bib.*

CLINE, Ray S
Secrets, spies and scholars: blueprint of the essential CIA *(Washington, DC: Acropolis 1976), 294p.*

DARLING, Donald
Sunday at large: assignments of a secret agent *(London: Kimber 1977), 174p.*
Previously published as: Secret Sunday

DUNLOP, Richard
Donovan, America's master spy *(New York: Rand McNally 1982), 562p.*

ELLIOTT-BATEMAN, M *ed.*
The fourth dimension of warfare: vol.I intelligence, subversion, resistance *(Manchester: Manchester UP 1970), 181p.*

EPPLER, John
Operation Condor: Rommel's spy *(London: Macdonald & Jane's 1977), 250p.*

HAESTRUP, Jorgen
Secret alliance *(Odense, Norway: Odense University 1976−7), 3 vols.*
Later published as: Europe ablaze

HAMILTON, A
Wings of night *(London: Kimber 1977), 206p.*

HUTCHISON, *Sir* James
Danger has no face *(London: Arrow 1978), 172p.*
Previously published as: That drug danger

JOHNSON, Stowers
Agents extraordinary *(London: Hale 1975), 192p.*

KATONA, Edita *and* MACNAGHTON, Patrick
Code-name Marianne *(London: Collins-Harvill 1976), 213p.*

MASSON, Madeleine
Christine: a search for Christine Granville, GM., OBE., Croix de Guerre *(London: Hamilton 1975), 263p., bib.*

MINSHALL, Merlin
Guild-edged *(London: Bachman & Turner 1975), 319p.*

MORAVEC, Frantisek
Master of spies: the memoirs of General Frantisek Moravec *(London: Bodley Head 1975), 252p.*

MURE, David
Master of deception: tangled webs in London and the Middle East *(London: Kimber 1980), 284p., bib.*
Practice to deceive *(London: Kimber 1977), 270p., bib.*

PAINE, Laurans
Mathilde Carre: double agent *(London: Hale 1976), 192p., bib.*

PEIS, Gunter
The mirror of deception: spies of the Third Reich *(London: Weidenfeld & Nicolson 1977), 190p., bib.*

PERSICO, Joseph E
Piercing the Reich: the penetration of Nazi Germany by American secret service agents during World War II *(New York: Viking 1979), 376p., bib.*

PITT, Roxane
Operation double life: an autobiography *(London: Bachman & Turner 1976), 183p.*

RADO, Sandor
Code name Dora *(London: Abelard 1977), 298p.*

READ, Anthony *and* FISHER, David
Operation Lucy: most secret spy ring of the Second World War *(London: Hodder & Stoughton 1980), 254p., bib.*

STEVENSON, William
A man called Intrepid *(London: Macmillan 1976), 486p.*

TREPPER, Leopold
The great game: the story of the Red Orchestra *(New York: McGraw-Hill 1976), 442p.*

VERITY, Hugh W
We landed by moonlight *(London: Ian Allan 1978), 256p.*

WEAVER, Richie
True spy stories of World War II *(London: Carousel 1975), 127p.*

WEST, Nigel
MI6: British secret intelligence service operations, 1909—1945 *(London: Weidenfeld & Nicolson 1983), 266p.*

WINTERBOTHAM, F W
The Nazi connection: the personal story of a top-level British agent in pre-war Germany *(London: Weidenfeld & Nicolson 1978), 222p.*
Secret and personal *(London: Kimber 1969), 192p.*

[*see also INTELLIGENCE, RESISTANCE*]

SECRET WEAPONS

BALDWIN, Ralph B
The deadly fuze: the secret weapon of World War II *(London: Macdonald & Jane's 1980), 332p.*

GARLINSKI, Jozef
Hitler's last weapons: the underground war against the V1 and V2 *(London: Friedman 1978), 244p., bib.*

HOGG, Ian Vernon *and* KING, J B
German and Allied secret weapons of World War II *(London: Phoebus 1976), 127p.*

SHEFFIELD

WALTON, Mary *comp.*
Raiders over Sheffield: the story of the air raids of 12th and 15th December 1940 *(Sheffield: City Libraries 1980), 169p.*

SICILY

CAMPBELL, Rodney
The Luciano project: the secret wartime collaboration of the Mafia and the U.S. Navy *(New York: McGraw-Hill 1977), 299p.*

COLE, *Sir* David
Rough road to Rome: a foot-soldier in Sicily and Italy, 1943–44 *(London: Kimber 1983), 239p.*

GARLAND, A *and* SMYTH, H
Sicily and the surrender of Italy *(Washington, DC: Dept of Army, 1965)*

PACK, S W C
Operation 'Husky': the Allied invasion of Sicily *(Newton Abbot, Devon: David & Charles 1977), 186p., bib.*

SINGAPORE

ALLEN, Louis
Singapore, 1941–1942 *(London: Davis-Poynter 1977), 343p., bib.*

BLOOM, Freddy
Dear Philip *(London: Bodley Head 1980), 160p.*

CAFFREY, Kate
Out in the midday sun *(London: Deutsch 1974), 312p., bib.*

CALLAHAN, Raymond
The worst disaster: the fall of Singapore *(Cranbury, NJ: University of Delaware 1977), 293p.*

CURLEWIS, Adrian
Of love and war: the letters and diaries of Captain Adrian Curlewis and his family, 1939—1945 *(Sydney, Aust: Lansdowne 1982), 280p.*

FRANKS, John
I fed the 5,000 *(London: Mitre 1975), 111p.*

HOLMES, Richard *and* KEMP, Anthony
The bitter end: the fall of Singapore, 1941—42 *(Chichester, Sx: Bird 1982), 250p.*

NELSON, David
The story of Changi Singapore *(Perth, W.Aust: Changi 1974), unp.*

SLIM

LEWIN, Ronald
Slim: the standardbearer *(London: Cooper 1976), 350p., bib.*

SOUTH AFRICA

MARTIN, Henry J *and* ORPEN, N D
South Africa at war: military and industrial organization and operations in connection with the conduct of war, 1939—1945 *(Cape Town: Purnell 1979), 405p.*

SOUTH AMERICA

FRANCIS, Michael J
The limits of hegemony: U.S. relations with Argentina and Chile during World War II *(Notre Dame, Ill: University of Notre Dame 1977), 292p.*

SOUTH EAST ASIA

BLAIR, Joan *and* BLAIR, Clay
Return from the River Kwai *(London: Macdonald & Jane's 1979), 338p.*

SPAIN

AVNI, Haim
Spain, the Jews and Franco *(New York: Jewish 1982), 268p.*

KLEINFELD, Gerald R *and* TAMBS, L
Hitler's Spanish Legion: the Blue Division in Russia *(Carbondale, Ill: Southern Illinois UP 1979), 434p.*

PROCTOR, Raymond L
Agony of a neutral: Spanish—German relations and the Blue Division *(Moscow, Idaho: Idaho Res. Foundation 1974), 359p.*

SPECIAL BOAT SERVICE

COURTNEY, G B
S.B.S.: the story of the Special Boat Service in World War II *(London: Hale 1983), 240p.*

PITT, Barrie
Special Boat Squadron: the story of the S.B.S. in the Mediterranean *(London: Century 1983), 192p.*

SPECIAL OPERATIONS EXECUTIVE (SOE)

BADEN-POWELL, Dorothy
Operation Jupiter: SOE's secret war in Norway *(London: Hale 1982), 208p., bib.*

BEEVOR, J G
SOE recollections and reflections, 1940—1945 *(London: Bodley Head 1981), 269p., bib.*

CRUICKSHANK, Charles
SOE in the Far East: Special Operations Executive *(London: OUP 1983), 285p.*

DAVIDSON, Basil
Special operations Europe: scenes from the anti-Nazi war *(London: Gollancz 1980), 288p., bib.*

DODDS-PARKER, *Sir* Douglas
Setting Europe ablaze *(London: Springwood 1983), 224p.*

FRANKS, Norman L R
Double mission: RAF fighter ace and SOE agent Manfred Czernin, DSO., MC., DFC. *(London: Kimber 1976), 192p.*

FULLER, Jean O
The German penetration of SOE: France 1941—1944 *(London: Kimber 1975), 192p.*

HOWARTH, Patrick
Undercover: the men and women of the Special Operations Executive *(London: Routledge & Kegan Paul 1980), 248p., bib.*

JOHNS, Philip
Within two cloaks: missions with SIS and SOE *(London: Kimber 1979), 216p.*

STAFFORD, David
Britain and European resistance, 1940—1945: a survey of the Special Operations Executive *(London: Macmillan 1980), 295p.*

TREVOR-ROPER, Hugh R
The Philby affair: espionage, treason and secret service *(London: Kimber 1968), 126p.*

[*see also SECRET SERVICE*]

STALIN

KUSNIERZ, Bronislaw
Stalin and the Poles: an indictment of the Soviet leaders
(Westport, Conn: Hyperion 1980), 317p.

SEATON, Albert
Stalin as warlord *(London: Batsford 1976), 312p., bib.*

STALINGRAD

KONSALIK, Heinz G
The heart of the 6th Army *(Henley-on-Thames, Oxon: Ellis 1977), 298p.*

[*see also GERMAN ARMY*]

STRATEGY

BARCLAY, Glen St J
Their finest hour: an original examination of British strategy in the early part of World War II *(London: Weidenfeld & Nicolson 1977), 192p., bib.*

COAKLEY, Robert W *and* LEIGHTON, Richard M
Global logistics and strategy, 1943—1945 *(Washington, DC: Dept of Army 1968), 889p.*

GRAND STRATEGY *(London: HMSO 1976), vol.I, 859p.*

GREENFIELD, Kent R
American strategy in World War II: a reconsideration *(Westport, Conn: Greenwood 1979), 145p.*

Command decisions *(London: Methuen 1960), 477p.*

HAYES, Grace P
The history of the Joint Chiefs of Staff in World War II: the war against Japan *(Annapolis, Md: Naval Institute 1982), 964p.*

IRVING, David
The war between the Generals *(London: Lane 1981), 446p.*

JACOBSEN, Hans A *and* SMITH, A L
World War II: policy and strategy *(Santa Barbara, Cal: Clio 1979), 505p.*

KENNETT, Lee
A history of strategic bombing *(New York: Scribner 1982), 222p.*

ROSTOW, W W
Pre-invasion bombing strategy *(Farnborough, Hants: Gower 1981), 176p.*

WILLMOTT, H P
Empires in the balance: Japanese and Allied Pacific strategies to April 1942 *(London: Orbis 1982), 487p., bib.*

SUBMARINES

BAGNASCO, Ermine
Submarines of World War II *(London: Arms & Armour 1977), 256p.*

BLAIR, Clay
Silent victory: the U.S. submarine war against Japan *(Philadelphia, Pa: Lippincott 1975), 1072p.*

CARR, Roland T
To sea in haste *(Washington, DC: Acropolis 1975), 260p.*

COMPTON-HALL, Richard
The underwater war, 1939—1945 *(Poole, Dorset: Blandford 1982), 160p.*

COOK, Graeme
Silent marauders *(London: Hart-Davis, MacGibbon 1976), 159p., bib.*

KING, William
Dive and attack: a submariner's story *(London: Kimber 1983)*

LOWDER, Hughston, E *and* SCOTT, Jack
Batfish, the champion submarine-killer submarine of World War II *(New York: Prentice-Hall 1980), 232p.*

SHAPIRO, Milton J
Undersea raiders: U.S. submarines in World War II *(New York: McKay 1979), 56p.*

STAFFORD, Edward P
The far and the deep *(New York: Putnam 1967), 382p.*

STERN, Robert C
U.S. submarines in action *(Carrollton, Tex: Squadron 1979), 43p.*

WALDRON, Thomas J *and* GLEESON, J J
Midget submarine *(New York: Ballantine 1975), 159p., bib.*

WHEELER, Keith
War under the Pacific *(Alexandria, Va: Time-Life 1980), 208p.*

SUMATRA

JACOBS, Gideon F
Prelude to the monsoon *(Cape Town: Purnell 1965), 247p.*

WARNER, Lavina *and* SANDILANDS, John
Women beyond the wire *(Feltham, Mx: Hamlyn 1983), 289p.*

SWEDEN

CARLGREN, W M
Swedish foreign policy during the Second World War *(London: Benn 1977), 257p., bib.*

LEWANDOWSKI, Josef
Swedish contribution to the Polish resistance movement during World War II *(Uppsala, Sweden: University of Uppsala 1979), 114p.*

SWITZERLAND

GARLINSKI, Jozef
   The Swiss corridor: espionage networks in Switzerland during World War II *(London: Dent 1981), 222p., bib.*

SCHWARZ, Urs
   The eye of the hurricane: Switzerland in World War Two *(Boulder, Col: Westview 1980), 169p.*

SYRIA

MOCKLER, Anthony
   Our enemies the French: an account of the war fought between the French and the British, Syria, 1941 *(London: Cooper 1976), 252p.*

TANKS

BAILY, Charles M
   Faint praise: American tanks and tank destroyers during World War II *(Hamden, Conn: Archon 1983), 196p.*

CHAMBERLAIN, Peter *and* ELLIS, Chris
   British and American tanks of World War Two: the complete illustrated history of British, American and Commonwealth tanks, gun motor carriages, and special purpose vehicles, 1939—1945 *(London: Arms & Armour 1971), 222p.*
   The Churchill tank: story of Britain's most famous tank, 1939—1965 *(London: Arms & Armour 1971), 110p.*
   The Sherman: an illustrated history of the M4 medium tank *(London: Arms & Armour 1968), 78p.*

CHAMBERLAIN, Peter *and* GANDER, Terence J
   American tanks of World War 2 *(Cambridge: Stephens 1977), 64p.*

172

CHAMBERLAIN, Peter *and* MILSOM, J
Allied combat tanks *(London: Macdonald & Jane's 1978)*, *64p.*

FORTY, George
United States tanks of World War II in action *(Poole, Dorset: Blandford 1983),* *160p.*

GANDER, Terence J *and* CHAMBERLAIN, Peter
British tanks of World War II *(Cambridge: Stephens 1976)*, *64p.*

GROVE, Eric
World War II tanks *(London: Orbis 1976), 143p.*

KREBS, John E
To Rome and beyond: battle adventures of Company B 760th Tank Battalion, Italy 1943—1945 *(Weatherford, Tex: Krebs 1981), 224p.*

MACKSEY, Kenneth
Tank tactics, 1939—1945 *(London: Almark 1976), 72p.*

PERRETT, Bryan
Allied tank destroyers *(London: Osprey 1979), 40p.*
The Churchill tank *(London: Osprey 1980), 40p.*
The Panzerkampfwagen III *(London: Osprey 1980), 40p.*
The Stuart light tank series *(London: Osprey 1980), 40p.*
Through mud and blood: infantry-tank operations in World War II *(London: Hale 1975), 272p., bib.*
The Tiger tanks *(London: Osprey 1981), 40p.*

SANDARS, John
Operation Crusader *(London: Almark 1976), 48p.*
The Sherman tank in British service, 1942—45 *(London: Osprey 1980), 40p.*

WARDROP, Jake
Tanks across the desert *(London: Kimber 1981), 222p., bib.*

WARNER, Philip
Panzer *(London: Weidenfeld & Nicolson 1977), 144p.*

WHITE, Brian T
Tanks and other armoured fighting vehicles, 1942—45 *(Poole, Dorset: Blandford 1975), 171p.*

ZALOGA, Steven J *comp.*
Battle of the Bulge *(London: Arms & Armour 1983), 63p.*
U.S. light tanks in action *(Carrollton, Tex: Squadron 1979), 49p.*

[*see also GERMAN ARMY PANZERS*]

TRANSPORT

BUNKER, John G
Liberty ship: the ugly duckling of World War II *(Annapolis, Md: Naval Institute 1972), 287p.*

ELLIS, Chris
Famous ships of World War 2 *(Poole, Dorset: Blandford 1976), 210p.*

KALLA-BISHOP, Peter M
Locomotives at war: Army railway reminiscences of the Second World War *(Truro, Cornwall: Barton 1980), 151p.*

TRIESTE

CAMPBELL, John C *ed.*
Successful negotiation, Trieste 1954: an appraisal by the five participants *(Princeton, NJ: Princeton UP 1976), 181p.*

COX, Geoffrey
The race for Trieste *(London: Kimber 1977), 284p.*

U-BOATS

BOTTING, Douglas S
The U-Boats *(Alexandria, Va: Time-Life 1979), 176p.*

BUCHHEIM, Lother-Gunther
U-Boat war *(London: Collins 1978), 304p.*

HOYT, Edwin P
U-Boats offshore *(New York: Playboy 1980), 285p.*

JONES, Geoffrey
The month of the lost U-Boats *(London: Kimber 1977), 207p.*

POOLMAN, Kenneth
The sea hunters *(London: Sphere 1982), 195p.*
Also published as: The sea hunters, escort carriers v.
U-Boats, 1941—1945

PRESTON, Anthony
U-Boats *(London: Arms & Armour 1978), 192p.*

PRICE, Alfred
Aircraft versus submarines *(London: Kimber 1973), 312p.*

SHOWELL, J P
U-Boats under the swastika: an introduction to German
submarines, 1935—1945 *(London: Arco 1977), 167p.*

U-BOATS In the Atlantic: a selection of German wartime
photographs *(Cambridge: Stephens 1979), 94p.*

WATTS, Anthony J
The U-Boat hunters *(London: Macdonald & Jane's 1976), 192p., bib.*

ULTRA

BELL, E L
Ultra as an American weapon *(New Hampshire: TSUP 1977)*

BENNETT, Ralph
Ultra in the West: the Normandy campaign of 1944
(London: Hutchinson 1979), 305p.

CALVOCORESSI, Peter
Top secret Ultra: the inside story of the British code-
breakers *(London: Cassell 1980), 144p.*

JOHNSON, Brian
The secret war *(London: BBC 1979), 352p.*

JONES, R V
Most secret war *(London: Hamilton 1978), 556p.*
US title: The wizard war

LEWIN, Ronald
The other Ultra *(London: Hutchinson 1982), 332p., bib.*
Ultra goes to war *(London: Hutchinson 1978), 398p., bib.*

MONTAGU, Ewen E S
Beyond top secret Ultra *(London: Davies 1977), 192p.*

WELCHMAN, Gordon
The hut six story: breaking the Enigmas *(London: Lane 1982), 328p., bib.*

[*see also* CODES AND CIPHERS, ENIGMA, PURPLE]

UNIFORMS

BENDER, Roger J *and* LAW, Richard D
Uniforms, organization and history of the Afrika Korps *(Mountain View: Bender 1973), 253p., bib.*

COOPER, Matthew
Uniforms of the Luftwaffe *(London: Almark 1974), 80p.*

DAVIS, Brian L
British Army uniforms and insignia of World War Two *(London: Arms & Armour 1983), 228p.*
Flags and standards of the Third Reich: Army, Navy and Air Force, 1933—1945 *(London: Macdonald & Jane's 1975), 160p.*
German ground forces, Poland and France, 1939—1940 *(London: Almark 1976), 72p.*
Luftwaffe air crews: Battle of Britain, 1940 *(London: Arms & Armour 1974), 33p.*

FUNCKEN, Liliane
Arms and uniforms: the Second World War *(London: Ward Lock 1975—76), 4 vols.*

MOLLO, Andrew
German uniforms of World War II *(London: Macdonald & Jane's 1976), 160p., bib.*
Naval, Marine and Air Force uniforms of World War II *(Poole, Dorset: Blandford 1975), 231p.*
Uniforms of the SS *(London: Historical Research Unit 1977), vol.I.*
World Army uniforms since 1939 *(Poole, Dorset: Blandford 1983)*

PIA, Jack
Nazi regalia *(New York: Ballantine 1971), unp.*

WILKINSON, Frederick J
A source book of World War 2 weapons and uniforms *(London: Ward Lock 1980), 128p.*

WINDROW, Martin C
World War Two combat uniforms and insignia *(Cambridge: Stephens 1977), 104p., bib.*

[see also ARMS AND ARMOUR]

UNITED STATES OF AMERICA (general)

BAILEY, Ronald H
The home front, USA *(Alexandria, Va: Time-Life 1977), 208p.*

BLUM, John M
V was for victory: politics and American culture during World War II *(New York: Harcourt 1976), 372p.*

CLIVE, Alan
State of war: Michigan in World War II *(Ann Arbor, Mich: University of Michigan 1979), 301p.*

COLE, Wayne S
Charles A. Lindbergh and the battle against American intervention in World War II *(New York: Harcourt 1974), 298p.*

EMMERSON, J K
The Japanese threat: a life in the U.S. foreign service *(New York: Holt 1978), 465p.*

FISH, Hamilton
FDR: the other side of the coin: how we were tricked into World War II *(New York: Vantage 1976), 255p.*

FOX, Frank W
Madison Avenue goes to war: the strange military career of American advertising, 1941—45 *(Salt Lake City, Utah: Brigham Young University 1975), 98p.*

GLABERMAN, Martin
Wartime strikes: the struggle against the no-strike pledge of the UAW during World War II *(Detroit, Mich: Bewick 1980), 158p.*

GUN, Nerin E
The day of the Americans *(New York: Fleet 1966), 317p.*

HEIFERMAN, Ronald *and others*
USA in World War II *(London: Hamlyn 1980), 384p.*

IRIYE, Akira
Power and culture: the Japanese—American war, 1941—1945 *(Cambridge, Mass: Harvard UP 1981), 304p., bib.*

ISSERMAN, Maurice
Which side were you on?: the American Communist Party during the Second World War *(Middletown, Conn: Wesleyan UP 1982), 305p.*

LINGEMAN, R
Don't you know there's a war on?: the American home front, 1941—1945 *(New York: Putnam 1970), 400p.*

MONTH Of infamy: December 1941 *(Culver City, Cal: Venture 1976), 144p.*

NEU, Charles E
The troubled encounter: the United States and Japan *(New York: Wiley 1975), 257p.*

PERRY, Glen C H
'Dear Bart': Washington views of World War II *(Westport, Conn: Greenwood 1982), 341p.*

PORTER, David L
The Seventy-sixth Congress and World War II *(Columbia, Mo: Missouri UP 1980), 236p., bib.*

SMYTH, Howard M
Secrets of the fascist era: how Uncle Sam obtained some of the top-level documents of Mussolini's period *(Carbondale, Ill: Southern Illinois UP 1979), 305p.*

STOLER, Mark A
The politics of the second front: American military planning and diplomacy in coalition warfare, 1941—1943 *(Westport, Conn: Greenwood 1977), 244p., bib.*

UNITED STATES ARMY (general)

BURHANS, Robert D
The First Special Service Force: a war history of the North Americans, 1942—1944 *(Nashville, Tenn: Battery 1981), 376p.*

HALE, Edwin R W *and* FRAYN, John
The Yanks are coming *(Tunbridge Wells, Kent: Courier 1983), 210p.*

KATCHER, Philip R N
The U.S. Army, 1941—45 *(London: Osprey 1978), 48p.*

KREBS, John E
To Rome and beyond *(Weatherford, Tex: Krebs 1981), 224p.*

LONGMATE, Norman
The G.I.'s: the Americans in Britain, 1942—1945 *(New York:Scribner 1976), 416p.*

MATHIAS, Frank F
G.I. Jive: an Army bandsman in World War II *(Lexington, Kty: University of Kentucky 1982), 227p.*

THE UNITED STATES ARMY In World War II *(Washington, DC: Dept of Army 1961), 14 vols*

WALKER, Wilbert L
We are men: memoirs of World War II *(Baltimore, Md: Heritage 1980), 129p.*

WHEELER, Keith
The road to Tokyo *(Alexandria, Va: Time-Life 1979), 208p.*

ZIEMKE, Earl F
The U.S. Army in the occupation of Germany *(Washington, DC: Dept of Army 1975)*

(Third Army)

FORTY, George
Patton's Third Army at war *(London: Ian Allan 1978), 192p.*

FRANKEL, Nathan *and* SMITH, L J
Patton's best: an informal history of the 4th Armoured Division *(Melbourne, Aust: Hawthorn 1978), 198p.*

McHUGH, Vernon O
From hell to heaven: memoirs from Patton's Third Army *(New York: Dorrance 1980), 95p.*

WALLACE, Brenton G
Patton and his Third Army *(Westport, Conn: Greenwood 1979), 232p.*

(Fifth Army)

FORTY, George
Fifth Army at war *(London: Ian Allan 1980), 144p., bib.*

(Sixth Army)

KRUEGER, Walter
  From down under to Nippon: the story of Sixth Army in
  World War II *(Washington, DC: Zenger 1979), 393p.*

(Seventh Army)

TURNER, John F *and* JACKSON, Robert
  Destination Berchtesgaden: the story of the U.S. 7th Army
  in World War II *(New York: Scribner 1975), 192p.*

(Divisions)

BALDWIN, Hanson W
  Tiger Jack (4th Armored Division) *(Fort Collins, Col:
  Old Army 1979), 198p.*

CASEWIT, Curtis W
  The saga of the mountain soldiers: the story of the 10th
  Mountain Division *(New York: Messner 1981), 159p.*

DAVIDSON, Orlando R
  The deadeyes: the story of the 96th Infantry Division
  (Nashville, Tenn: Battery 1981), 310p.

A HISTORY Of the United States Twelfth Armored
  Division: 15th Sept. 1942—17th December 1945
  (Nashville, Tenn: Battery 1978), 93p.

KATCHER, Philip R N
  U.S. 1st Infantry Division, 1939—45 *(London: Osprey
  1978), 40p.*
  U.S. 2nd Armored Division 1979 *(London: Osprey 1979),
  40p.*
  3rd Armored Division, spearhead in the West *(Nashville,
  Tenn: Battery 1980)*

LOVE, Edmund G
The 27th Infantry Division in World War II *(Washington, DC: Infantry Journal 1949), 677p.*

TANAKA, Chester
Go for broke: a pictorial history of the Japanese—American 100th Infantry Battalion, and the 442nd Regimental Combat Team *(Richmond, Cal: Go for Broke 1982), 172p.*

WHITING, Charles
Death of a Division (106th Infantry Division) *(London: Cooper 1979), 158p., bib.*

UNITED STATES ARMY AIR FORCE

BIRDSALL, Steve
Flying buccaneers: the illustrated story of Kenney's Fifth Air Force *(New York: Doubleday 1977), 312p.*
Saga of the Superfortress: the dramatic story of the B.29 and the Twentieth Air Force *(London: Sidgwick & Jackson 1982), 346p.*

BOWMAN, Martin
Fields of little America: an illustrated history of the 8th Air Force, 2nd Division, 1942—45 *(Norwich, Norfolk: Wensum 1977), 128p.*

COFFEY, Thomas M
Decision over Schweinfurt: the U.S. 8th Air Force battle for daylight bombing *(London: Hale 1978), 373p.*

ETHELL, Jeffrey
American warplanes: World War Two—Korea *(London: Arms & Armour 1983), 2 vols*

FRANCILLON, Rene J
USAAF fighter units: Europe 1942—45 *(London: Osprey 1977), 48p.*

FREEMAN, Roger A *and others*
Mighty Eighth war diary *(London: Jane's 1981), 508p.*

HOSEASON, James
The 1000 day battle *(Lowestoft, Suffolk: Gillingham 1979), 256p., bib.*

HOWARD, Clive *and* WHITLEY, J
One damned island after another: the saga of the 7th Air Force in World War II *(Washington, DC: Zenger 1979), 403p.*

INFIELD, Glenn B
Big week *(New York: Pinnacle 1974), 218p.*

IVIE, Thomas G
Aerial reconnaissance: the 10th Photo Reconnaissance Group in World War II *(Fallbrook, Cal: Aero 1981), 200p.*

JACKSON, Robert
The secret squadrons *(London: Robson 1983), 192p.*

JOHNSEN, Frederik A
The bomber barons: the history of the 5th Bomb Group in the Pacific during World War II *(Tacoma, Wash: Bomber 1982), vol.I*

McCRARY, John R *and* SCHERMAN, D C
First of the many: a journal of action with the men of the Eighth Air Force *(London: Robson 1981), 241p.*

MacISAAC, David
Strategic bombing in World War II: the story of the United States strategic bombing survey *(London: Garland 1976), 231p., bib.*

MONDEY, David *and* NALLS, L
USAAF at war in the Pacific *(London: Ian Allan 1980), 160p.*

MORRIS, Danny
Aces and wingmen: men, machines and units of the United States Army Air Force, Eighth Fighter Command in 354th Fighter Group, Ninth Air Force, 1943—45 *(London: Spearman 1975), 489p.*

MORRISON, Wilbur H
Point of no return *(New York: Playboy 1980), 261p.*

MUNSON, Kenneth G
American aircraft of World War 2 in colour *(Poole, Dorset: Blandford 1982), 160p.*

MUSCIANO, Walter A
Corsair aces, the bent wing bird over the Pacific *(New York: Arco 1979), 136p.*

NEWBY, Leroy W
Target Ploesti: view from a bombsight *(London: Arms & Armour 1983), 288p.*

OSUR, Alan M
Blacks in the Army Air Force during World War II *(New York: Arno 1980), 227p.*

RUST, Kenn C
Eighth Air Force story in World War II *(Temple City, Cal: Historical Aviation Album 1978), 78p.*
Fifteenth Air Force story in World War II *(London: Hessant 1976), 64p.*
Fourteenth Air Force story in World War II *(Temple City, Cal: Historical Aviation Album 1977), 64p.*
Seventh Air Force story in World War II *(Temple City, Cal: Historical Aviation Album 1979), 64p.*
Tenth Air Force story in World War II *(Glendale, Cal: Aviation 1980), 64p.*

RUST, Kenn C *and* BELL, D
Thirteenth Air Force story in World War II *(London: Hessant 1981), 64p.*

SHORES, Christopher F
USAAF fighter units MTO, 1943–45 *(London: Osprey 1978), 48p.*

SIEFRING, Thomas A
US Air Force in World War II *(London: Hamlyn 1978), 192p.*

SPIGHT, Edwin L *and* SPIGHT, J L
Eagles of the Pacific: memoirs of an air transport service during World War II *(Glendale, Cal: Aviation 1980), 224p.*

UNITED STATES DEPT of the Office of Air Force History
Army Air Forces in World War II *(Washington, DC: 1948–1951), 7 vols.*

UNITED STATES MARINE CORPS

BARROW, Jess C
World War II Marine Fighting Squadron Nine (VF-9M)
(New York: TAB 1981), 239p.

DEAR, Ian
Marines at war *(London: Ian Allan 1982), 128p.*

DE CHANT, John A
Devil birds: the story of the U.S. Marine Corps aviation in
World War II *(Washington, DC: Zenger 1979), 265p.*

DOWNEY, Bill
Uncle Sam must be losing the war: black Marines of 51st
(San Francisco, Cal: Strawberry Hill 1982), 217p.

FOSS, Joseph J
Joe Foss, flying Marine: the story of his flying circus in
World War II *(Washington, DC: Zenger 1979), 160p.*

JOSEPHY, Alvin
The long and the short and the tall: the story of a Marine
combat unit in the Pacific *(Washington, DC: Zenger 1979),
221p.*

OLYNYK, Frank J
USMC credits for the destruction of enemy aircraft in air-
to-air combat in World War 2 *(Aurora, Ohio: Olynyk
1981), 214p.*

RICHARDSON, W
The epic of Tarawa *(London: Odhams 1945), 96p.*

SIMMONS, E H
The United States Marines *(London: Cooper 1974), 184p.*

185

WHEELER, Richard
Of special valor: the U.S. Marines and the Pacific war *(New York: Harper 1983), 466p.*

[*see also BATAAN, CORREGIDOR, PACIFIC, PHILIPPINES*]

UNITED STATES NAVY

ABBAZIA, Patrick
Mr Roosevelt's Navy: the private war of the U.S. Atlantic Fleet, 1939–1945 *(Annapolis, Md: Naval Institute 1975), 520p.*

ANDERTON, David A
Hellcat *(London: Macdonald & Jane's 1981), 56p.*

HEIFERMAN, Ronald
US Navy in World War II *(London: Hamlyn 1978), 192p.*

HOLMES, Wilfred J
Double-edged secrets: U.S. Naval intelligence operations in the Pacific during World War II *(Annapolis, Md: Naval Institute 1979), 231p.*

HOYT, Edwin P
The lonely ships: the life and death of the U.S. Asiatic Fleet *(New York: McKay 1976), 338p.*

LECH, Raymond R
All the drowned sailors *(New York: Stein & Day 1982), 309p.*

LENTON, Henry T
American gunboats and minesweepers *(London: Macdonald & Jane's 1974), 64p.*

MASON, Theodore C
Battleship sailor *(Annapolis, Md: Naval Institute 1983), 352p.*

MESSINER, Dwight R
Pawns of war: the loss of the USS Langley and the USS Pecos *(Annapolis, Md: Naval Institute 1983), 248p.*

O'LEARY, Michael
United States Naval fighters of World War II in action *(Poole, Dorset: Blandford 1980), 160p., bib.*

REILLY, John C
United States Navy destroyers of World War II *(Poole, Dorset: Blandford 1983), 160p.*

TILLMAN, Barret
Avenger at war *(London: Ian Allan 1979), 128p.*

TOLLEY, Kemp
The cruise of the Lanikai: incitement to war *(Annapolis, Md: Naval Institute 1973), 346p.*

[*see also PACIFIC, PEARL HARBOR, SUBMARINES*]

VATICAN

MORLEY, John F
Vatican diplomacy and the Jews during the holocaust *(New York: Ktav 1980), 327p.*

VICHY

MARRUS, Michael R *and* PAXTON, R O
Vichy France and the Jews *(London: Basic 1981), 442p.*

PAXTON, Robert O
Vichy France: old guard and new order *(Irvington, NY: Columbia 1982), 399p.*

[*see also FRANCE, JEWS*]

VICTORIA CROSS

BOWYER, Chaz
For valour: the air V.C.'s *(London: Kimber 1978), 548p.*

PHILLIPS, Cecil E L
Victoria Cross battles of the Second World War *(London: Pan 1976), 292p.*

WAR CRIMES

AITKEN, Leslie
Massacre on the road to Dunkirk: Wormhout, 1940 *(London: Kimber 1977), 189p., bib.*

HENRY, Clarissa *and* HILLEL, Marc
Children of the SS *(London: Hutchinson 1976), 256p.* US title: Of pure blood

KNOOP, Hans
The Menten affair *(London: Robson 1979), 109p.*

LOFTUS, John
The Belarus secret *(New York: Knopf 1982), 196p.*

MICHELSON, Frida
I survived Rumbuli *(New York: Scribner 1982), 232p.*

PEARSON, Michael
Tears of glory: the betrayal of Vercours, 1944 *(London: Macmillan 1978), 254p., bib.*

PICCIGAILO, Philip R
The Japanese on trial: Allied crime operations in the East, 1945—1951 *(Austin, Tex: University of Texas 1979), 292p.*

SHIROYAMA, Saburo
War criminal: the life and death of Hirota Koki *(Tokyo: Kodansha 1977), 301p.*

[*see also JEWS, POLAND, PRISON CAMPS*]

WARSAW

BOGUSLANSKA, Anna
Food for the children *(London: Cooper 1975), 201p.*

GUTMAN, Yisrael
The Jews of Warsaw, 1939—1943: ghetto, underground revolt *(Brighton, Sx: Harvester 1982), 487p., bib.*

HANSON, Joanna K M
The civilian population and the Warsaw uprising of 1944
(Cambridge: CUP 1982), 345p.

KULSKI, Julian E
Dying we live: the personal chronicle of a young street
fighter in Warsaw, 1939—1945 *(New York: Holt 1979),
304p.*

STROOP, Juergen
The Stroop report: the Jewish quarter of Warsaw is no
more *(London: Secker & Warburg 1980), 234p.*

ZAWODNY, Janusz K
Nothing but honour: the story of the Warsaw uprising,
1944 *(London: Macmillan 1978), 328p., bib.*

ZUKER-BUJANOWSKA, Liliana
Liliana's journal: Warsaw, 1939—1945 *(New York: Dial
1980), 162p.*

WAR TRIALS

BOSCH, William J
Judgement in Nuremberg: American attitudes toward the
major German war-crime trials *(Chapel Hill, NC: North
Carolina UP 1970), 272p.*

HEYDECKER, Joe J *and* LEEB, J
The Nuremberg trial: a history of Nazi Germany as re-
vealed through the testimony at Nuremberg *(New York:
Greenwood 1976), 348p.*

SMITH, Bradley F
Reaching judgment at Nuremberg *(London: Deutsch
1977), 354p.*

SPEER, Albert
Spandau: the secret diaries *(London: Collins 1976), 465p.*

WEBB, A M *ed.*
The Natzweiler trial *(London: Hodge 1949), 233p.*

WAVELL

FERGUSSON, Bernard
Wavell: portrait of a soldier *(London: Collins 1961), 96p.*

LEWIN, Ronald
The Chief: Field Marshal Lord Wavell, Commander-in-Chief, Viceroy, 1939—1947 *(London: Hutchinson 1980), 282p.*

WEAPONS

BARKER, Arthur J
British and American infantry weapons of World War Two *(London: Arms & Armour 1969), 76p.*
German infantry weapons of World War Two *(London: Arms & Armour 1969), 76p.*
Russian infantry weapons of World War Two *(London: Arms & Armour 1971), 80p.*

CARTER, J A
Allied bayonets of World War Two *(London: Arms & Armour 1969), 80p.*

[*see also ARMS AND ARMOUR*]

WESTERN EUROPE 1939—1940

BELL, Philip M H
A certain eventuality: Britain and the fall of France *(Farnborough, Hants: Saxon House 1974), 320p., bib.*

BEUS, J G de
Tomorrow at dawn *(New York: Norton 1980), 191p., bib.*

BOND, Brian
France and Belgium, 1939—1940 *(London: Davis-Poynter 1975), 206p., bib.*

KARSLAKE, Basil
1940, the last act: the story of the British Forces in France after Dunkirk *(London: Cooper 1979), 283p.*

PARKINSON, Roger
Dawn on our darkness *(London: Granada 1977), 236p., bib.*

RUTHERFORD, Ward
Blitzkrieg 1940 *(New York: Putnam 1980), 191p.*

SCHACHTMAN, Tom
The phoney war 1939 to 1940 *(New York: Harper 1982), 289p.*

WESTERN EUROPE 1944—1945

ALLEN, Peter
One more river: the Rhine crossings of 1945 *(London: Dent 1980), 326p., bib.*

BEUS, Jacobus G de
Tomorrow at dawn *(New York: Norton 1980), 191p.*

DAVIS, Franklin M
Across the Rhine *(Alexandria, Va: Time-Life 1980), 208p.*

FORTY, George
Desert Rats at war: 2, Europe *(London: Ian Allan 1977), 160p.*

GRIGG, John
1943: the victory that never was *(London: Eyre Methuen 1980), 255p., bib.*

KEMP, Anthony
The unknown battle: Metz 1944 *(New York: Stein & Day 1979), 261p., bib.*

LOVAT, Simon C J *17th baron*
March past: a memoir *(London: Weidenfeld & Nicolson 1978), 397p.*

MILLER, M
The far shore: an account of the American beachheads in Normandy, Southern France and Salerno *(New York: McGraw-Hill 1945), 173p.*

NORTH, John
North-West Europe, 1944—1945: the achievement of 21st Army Group *(London: HMSO 1953), 270p.*

RAWLING, Gerald
Cinderella operation: the battle of Walcheren, 1944 *(London: Cassell 1980), 164p., bib.*

SEATON, Albert
The fall of fortress Europe 1943—1945 *(London: Batsford 1981), 218p., bib.*

WEIGLY, Russell F
Eisenhower's lieutenants: the campaign of France and Germany, 1944—1945 *(London: Sidgwick & Jackson 1981), 800p.*

WELSH, Douglas
The U.S.A. in World War 2: the European theater *(New York: Galahad 1982), 64p.*

WHITING, Charles
Bloody Aachen *(London: Cooper 1976), 159p.*
Siegfried: the Nazis' last stand *(New York: Stein & Day 1982), 268p.*

[*see also AIRBORNE FORCES, COMMANDOS, D-DAY, FALAISE, NORMANDY*]

WOMEN

ANDERSON, Karen
Wartime women: sex roles, family relations, and the status of women during World War II *(Westport, Conn: Greenwood 1981), 198p.*

CASSIN-SCOTT, Jack
Women at war, 1939—1945 *(London: Osprey 1980), 40p.*

HIBBERT, Joyce K *ed.*
The war brides *(Toronto: Martin 1978), 160p.*

JACKSON, Robert
Heroines of World War II *(London: Barker 1976), 169p.*

KEIL, Sally
Those wonderful women in their flying machines: the unknown heroines of World War II *(New York: Rawson 1979), 334p.*

SIM, Kevin
Women at war: five heroines who defied the Nazis and survived *(New York: Morrow 1982), 286p.*

WILLIAMS, Eve
Ladies without lamps *(London: Harmsworth 1983), 178p.*

YUGOSLAVIA

AUTY, Phyllis *and* CLOGG, R
British policy towards wartime resistance in Yugoslavia and Greece *(London: Barnes & Noble 1975), 308p.*

DJILAS, Milovan
Wartime *(London: Secker & Warburg 1977), 470p.*

IVANOVIC, Vani
LX: memoirs of a Yugoslav *(London: Weidenfeld & Nicolson 1977), 435p.*

LASIC-VASOJEVIC, Milija M
Enemies on all sides: the fall of Yugoslavia *(Washington, DC: North American Institute 1976), 290p.*

MARTIN, David
Mihajlovic: patriot or traitor *(Stanford, Cal: Stanford UP 1979), 499p.*

MILAZZO, Matteo J
The Chetnik movement and the Yugoslav resistance *(Baltimore, Md: Johns Hopkins UP 1975), 208p.*

TOMASEVICH, Jozo
The Chetniks *(Stanford, Cal: Stanford UP 1975), 508p.*

AUTHOR INDEX

Author Index

Bailey, Dan E., *World War II wrecks of the Kwajalein and Truk lagoons*, 135

Bailey, R.H., *The air war in Europe*, 12; *The home front, USA*, 177

Bailey, T.A. & Ryan, P.B., *Hitler versus Roosevelt*, 124

Baily, C.M., *Faint praise*, 172

Baird, J.W., *The mythical world of Nazi war propaganda, 1939–1945*, 148

Baldwin, H.W., *The crucial years, 1939–1941*, 93; *Tiger Jack*, 181

Baldwin, Ralph B., *The deadly fuze*, 164

Balfour, M.L.G., *Propaganda war, 1939–1945*, 148

Ball, A., *The last day of the old world*, 93

Bancroft, M., *Autobiography of a spy*, 162

Barbarski, K., *Polish armour, 1939–45*, 15

Barber, N., *The week France fell*, 76

Barclay, George, *Fighter pilot*, 70

Barclay, Glen St. J., *Their finest hour*, 169

Barker, Arthur J., *Afrika Korps*, 7; *British and American infantry weapons of World War Two*, 190; *Dunkirk*, 62; *German infantry weapons of World War Two*, 190; *Japanese Army handbook, 1939–1945*, 107; *Ju-87 Stuka*, 81; *Panzers at war*, 86; *Russian infantry weapons of World War Two*, 190; *Waffen SS at war*, 87; *Yamashita*, 107

Barker, Elizabeth, *British policy in South-East Europe in the Second World War*, 59; *Churchill and Eden at war*, 59

Barker, Rachel, *Conscience, government and war*, 53

Barker, Ralph, *Against the sea*, 105; *The blockade busters*, 27; *The Hurricane*, 70; *The RAF at war*, 155

Barrington-Whyte, J., *The great tribulation*, 35

Barrow, J.C., *World War II Marine Fighting Squadron Nine (VF-9M)*, 185

Bartlett, B.R., *Cover-up*, 138

Basansky, B. & Manuel, D., *Babunia*, 160

Batchelor, J., *Fighting ships of World War One and Two*, 124

Bates, M.B., *A wilderness of days*, 17

Baty, J.A., *Surgeon in the jungle war*, 38, 119

Baudot, M., *The historical encyclopaedia of World War II*, 66

Bauer, Eddy, *The history of World War II*, 93

Bauer, Yehuda, *American Jewry and the holocaust*, 110; *From diplomacy to resistance*, 110; *The holocaust in perspective*, 110; *The Jewish emergence from powerlessness*, 110

Baumont, M., *The origins of the Second World War*, 134

Bavousett, G.B., *More World War II aircraft in combat*, 12

Bayfield, T., *Churban*, 110

Bayliss, G.M., *Bibliographic guide to the two World Wars*, 26

Beach, G.R., *The task supreme*, 35

Beaton, C., *War photographs*, 142

Beauman, A.B., *Then a soldier*, 139

Beaumont, J., *Comrades in arms*, 33

Beaumont, R., *Phoenix into ashes*, 155

Beaumont, Winifred H., *A detail on the Burma front*, 38

Beaver, P., *E-boats and coastal craft*, 64

Becton, F.J., & Morschauser, J., *The ship that would not die*, 124

Beekman, A., *The Niihau incident*, 92

Beesly, P., *Very special intelligence*, 99

Beeson, G., *Five roads to Dresden*, 146

Beevor, J.G., *SOE recollections and reflections, 1940–1945*, 168

Belchem, D., *All in the day's march*, 129; *Victory in Normandy*, 127

196

Author Index

200

Author Index

Author Index

Author Index

Author Index

Author Index

Author Index

214

Author Index

216

Author Index

Author Index

INDEX OF TITLED BOOKS ONLY

SUBJECT INDEX

224

Subject Index

225